TRADERS AND HEROES

WERNER SOMBART

TRADERS AND HEROES

PATRIOTIC REFLECTIONS

Translated with a Foreword by Alexander Jacob

ARKTOS
LONDON 2021

ARKTOS
⊕ Arktos.com   fb.com/Arktos   @arktosmedia   arktosmedia

Copyright © 2021 by Arktos Media Ltd.

All rights reserved. No part of this book may be reproduced or utilised in any form or by any means (whether electronic or mechanical), including photocopying, recording or by any information storage and retrieval system, without permission in writing from the publisher.

ISBN
978-1-914208-32-4 (Paperback)
978-1-914208-33-1 (Hardback)
978-1-914208-34-8 (Ebook)

Translation
Alexander Jacob

Editing
Constantin von Hoffmeister

Layout & Cover
Tor Westman

Proofreading
Alexis Jenners

CONTENTS

Foreword by Alexander Jacob vii

INTRODUCTION
The Religious War 1

PART ONE
English Traders

The Features of the English Mind 7
English Science 13
The English State and English Culture 27

PART TWO
German Heroism

The German Mind 41
The German Idea of the Fatherland 53
The German Idea of the State 59
German Militarism 67

PART THREE
The Mission of the German Nation

Life before the War 79
Desperate Rescue Attempts 87
The Redemption from the Evil 93
We and the Others 103

FOREWORD

BY ALEXANDER JACOB

WERNER SOMBART (1863–1941), the German economist and social philosopher, is noted today for his several pioneering works on the capitalistic ethos. Although Sombart began his sociological career as a socialist in the Marxist vein, he gradually dissociated himself from the economic orientation of Marx's social theory in favour of a more voluntarist understanding of the springs of social evolution which supported the traditional and aristocratic model of society that Marx had sought to destroy.

In his *Die deutsche Volkswirtschaft im neunzehnten Jahrhundert* (1903), Sombart turned his back on the socialist glorification of progress, which he saw as destructive of the human spirit, and revived the mediaeval ideal of the guild community, which involved, as Arthur Mitzman summarises it, "the full absorption and development of the personality of the producer in his work; limited goals; and the shaping of the productive units on the model of the family community".[1] The replacement of this original organic society by the artificial *Gesellschaft*, to use Tönnies' terminology, was consolidated, according to Sombart, by interferences in Germanic society, marked by abstract

---

1   See Arthur Mitzman, *Sociology and Estrangement: Three Sociologists of Imperial Germany*, N.Y.: Alfred A. Knopf, 1973, p. 194.

thoughts which were "synonymous with indifference towards qualitative values, with the inability to appreciate the concrete, individual, personal, living".² The symbolic expression of this abstraction was money, in which "all the qualitative values of consumer goods are dissolved and appear only in quantitative determination".³ The proletariat, which is the typical social product of capitalism, is the element which suffers most in the replacement of the patriarchal social ethos by the commercial, for "every community of interest is dissolved, as also every community of labour" and "bare payment is the only bond which ties the contracting parties together".⁴ The traditional popular comfort of religion too has been destroyed by capitalism, which bolstered the liberal intellectual movements of the Enlightenment.

In *Händler und Helden* (Munich, 1915), written to inspire young German soldiers in their combat against the English forces, Sombart considers the World War, started in Central Europe in July 1914, to be essentially one between England and Germany.⁵ For it is, in his view, an ideological, or even 'religious', war between the English worldview and the German one. The sociological and cultural significance of the war, according to Sombart, is the radical difference existing between the English "trader spirit", which aims at achieving mere "happiness" through the negative virtues of "temperance, contentedness, industry, sincerity, fairness, austerity … humility, patience, etc.", all of which will facilitate a "peaceful cohabitation of traders", and the "heroic spirit" of the Germans, which aims at fulfilling the mission of the higher self-realisation of humanity through the positive, 'giving' virtues of "the will to sacrifice, loyalty, guilelessness, reverence, bravery, piety,

2   Werner Sombart, *Die deutsche Volkswirtschaft im neunzehnten Jahrhundert*, Berlin: G. Bondi, 1903 (my translation).
3   *Ibid.*
4   Werner Sombart, *Das Proletariat*, Berlin: Rütten und Loening, 1906, p. 59 (my translation).
5   Germany joined forces with Austria-Hungary against Russia in August 1914, and Britain declared war against Germany when the latter invaded Belgium in the same month in order to gain access to France.

obedience, goodness" — as well as the 'military virtues', for "all heroism first fully develops in war and through war".⁶

War for the English has always been a chiefly commercial enterprise, whereas for the German it is a defence of his soul from the deadening influence of this same commercial spirit. In order to reveal the essential mercantile nature of the English nation, as well as of the war that they had recently embarked on in Europe, Sombart first points to the fact that the English have, through the ages, had no higher philosophy than a utilitarian and eudaimonistic one.⁷ This is demonstrable by a perusal of the works of the major English thinkers from the Elizabethan empiricist Francis Bacon (1561–1626) to the more recent evolutionary biologist and sociologist Herbert Spencer (1820–1903). Bacon's utilitarian views are geared to the acquisition of comfort as a source of human happiness. And it is this desire for comfort that, according to Sombart, informed the British trading enterprises around the world from the beginning of the 16th century onward, which, in turn, consolidated the mercantile mentality of the British nation as a whole.

Herbert Spencer's evolutionary sociological division of the history of societies into two major types, the militant and the industrial, is another device employed by the British to elevate the industrial society, focused on the same goal of comfort, above the militant. According to Spencer, the militant society is inferior because it generally posits violent actions as a national norm and 'deadens the sympathies' of its citizens, whereas the industrial society encourages 'altruistic sentiments and the resulting virtues'.⁸

---

6   Werner Sombart, *Händler und Helden: Patriotische Besinnungen*, Munich: Duncker und Humblot, 1915.

7   Sombart particularly recalls Nietzsche's similar low evaluation of the English mind and its typical representatives: 'They are not a philosophical race, these English. Bacon signifies an attack on the philosophical spirit in general, Hobbes, Hume and Locke a degradation and devaluation of the concept of a "philosopher" for more than a century.'

8   See *Principles of Sociology*, Art. 575.

The militant society, according to Spencer, is focused on a society's concern to preserve itself against hostile societies and nations to such a degree that all of society revolves around the military class and even those who do not bear arms (the 'workers') are forced to sustain the former. All individuals, however, are subservient to the state that acts as the guardian of the society as a whole. 'The life, the actions and the possessions of each individual must be held at the service of the society' (*Principles of Sociology*, Art. 561). The state is centralised and all of society organised in a hierarchical manner. Private commercial or social corporations are generally discouraged while the state pursues autarkic and protectionist economic policies. Spencer points to the German Empire of 1871 in particular as an example of a militant society where the army has been steadily strengthened to control national industry, and civil officialism has been replaced by military officialism. Bravery and strength are considered to be ideal individual virtues, since these are necessary for success in war, while patriotism and a sense of 'revenge' against those who harm it form the supreme social virtues of a militant society.

In an industrial society, on the other hand, the individuals do not work for corporate aims but for their own individual ones to the degree that the individual's individuality has to be defended by the society instead of being sacrificed to the latter as in the case of a militant society. Since the task of external protection is diminished in an industrial society, the state is more focused on preserving the life, liberty and property of its citizens. No longer organised from above as in a militant society (as well as in a communistic one, which shares in the same compulsory cooperation of the citizens), the industrial society operates not on the principle of 'status' but on that of 'contract', whereby each person is rewarded according to his merits. The state can no longer be centralised and the scope of its administration of the lives of the citizens is increasingly reduced. Among individuals, the industrial society fosters a sense of independence and diminishes those of patriotism and loyalty to any superior authority. There is a concomitant proliferation of individual associations of a mercantile and social nature. Finally, with the spread of industrialisation, the antagonisms between nations too are subsumed under the larger interests of international trade.

But Sombart considers the industrial society extolled by Spencer as a contemptible product of bourgeois individuals, who are devoted to their personal comfort, and of merchants, who desire peaceful relations between nations only in order to expand their private businesses. The British Empire, built on these considerations, is itself only a mechanical aggregation of commercial interests and is not informed by any ideal civilisatory impulses. The wars conducted by the British are also essentially trade wars, which seek to punish violations of the 'contracts' established by them with other nations for their international commercial purposes. Sombart points out in this context that one of the principal causes of the first international war was Britain's need to eliminate the threat posed by German industry to its colonial empire.

In the second part of *Händler und Helden,* Sombart points to the philosophical superiority of the Germans to the British. He reveals that, contrary to the history of British philosophy, the entire tendency of German philosophy, from the Romantics of the 18th century to the idealists of the 19th, has been one that posits a transcendental world of spirit above that of the individual on earth. It is this consciousness of participation in a higher world that gives German man a higher purpose than the limited eudaimonistic and utilitarian ones that have preoccupied the English thinkers.

The supraindividual scope of man is most fully represented by the nation to which he belongs, for the nation is the guarantor of the fullest development of the personality of the individuals constituting it. Nationalism thus achieves a soteriological significance through its metaphysical import. The organised body of the nation is the state, which has an organic quality, which Spencer had wrongly attributed to societies.⁹ As such, a state is capable of growth and must necessarily expand in the course of its development. This is the reason of wars, as Adam Müller (1779–1829) had pointed out, for, in every state there lives 'an inner pressure towards vital growth, fully unconscious to the present generation but deriving from the impetus of earlier generations'.¹⁰ A state that is constantly prepared for war necessarily has a militaristic quality, which is what the British thinkers like Spencer, as well as British propagandists during the war, had decried as a cardinal sin of Germany's.

But Sombart adduces the writings of Heinrich von Treitschke (1834–1896), the German historian and politician who championed the Prussian Hohenzollerns and Bismarck, to justify Germany's militarism. For Treitschke the state is only 'the framework of all national life'¹¹ and must be bolstered by military power, since war is a permanent concomitant of the state. War, though painful, is indeed conducive to curtailing the selfish obsessions of the individual. As he pointed out, every nation,

> most of all a finely-formed one, will fall victim easily in a long period of peace to weakening and selfishness. The unlimited comfort of society is the downfall not only of the state but at the same time of all the ideal wealth of life. The bourgeois mentality or cosmopolitan activity, which has in view only the satisfaction of all the pleasures of the individual, undermines

---

9   Houston Stewart Chamberlain (1855–1927) also published a wartime work *Politische Ideale* in the same year as Sombart's *Händler und Helden,* in which he defended the German social ethos with the same doctrine of the state as the arena in which man fully realises his humanity. The ideal state, according to Chamberlain, must be infused with a sense of Kantian inner freedom, and its self-discipline will resemble that of the German Army, where all the soldiers are united unto death for the achievement of the same national goal (see my English edition of this work, Houston Stewart Chamberlain, *Political Ideals,* Lanham, MD: University Press of America, 2005).
10 Adam Müller, *Die Elemente der Staatskunst,* Erste Vorlesung.
11 Heinrich von Treitschke, *Politics,* I, p. 54.

the foundations of a higher moral worldview and the belief in ideals. Superficial minds come to the nonsense that the life-purpose of the individual is acquisition and enjoyment, that the purpose of the state is nothing but the lightening of the business of its citizens, that man is destined to sell at a high price and buy cheap, that war, which disturbs him in this activity, is the greatest evil and the modern army only a sad relic of mediaeval barbarism.[12]

War thus has a therapeutic power in awakening the supraindividual ideal that lies latent in the citizens:

> As soon as the state calls out, 'Now it is a question of me and my existence', there awakens in a free people the highest of all virtues that cannot prevail in such a great and unrestricted way in peacetime: self-sacrifice ... The conflict of parties and classes yields to a sacred silence; even the thinker and artist feels that his ideal creation would only be a tree without roots if the state were to collapse. Among the thousands who go to war and selflessly obey the will of the whole, everyone knows how miserably little his life is worth next to the glory of the nation.[13]

Indeed, Treitschke even goes so far as to say, 'Without war no state could be'. By this he means also the state's civilisatory mission, for the 'great strides which civilization makes against barbarism and unreason are only made actual by the sword'.[14]

In the last section of *Händler und Helden*, Sombart, like Treitschke, points to Germany's real mission in the First World War, which is to restore the primacy of the idealistic heroic worldview against the paltry mercantile one of the British. Before the war, Germany itself had succumbed to an alarming degree to the eudaimonistic seductions of the British worldview with its stress on 'comfort' and the substitution of 'sports' for military discipline.

---

12   Treitschke, 'Das constitutionelle Königthum in Deutschland'.
13   Ibid.
14   Ibid., 65.

After discounting the ability of contemporary religion (including newly founded cults) to renovate German culture, Sombart pauses to examine the career of socialism as a regenerative social force. He points out that the communitarian idealism of socialism too has been distorted in a materialistic direction, since the comfortable life of the worker has taken precedence over national development. In other words, the revolutionary zeal of the socialists of the revolutions of 1848 and 1905 in Germany and Russia has been dissipated, and a loss of militancy is, in general (as Treitschke too had pointed out), a sign of a dilution of idealism.

Finally, Sombart declares that all 'humanitarian' ideals in general are illusory since they do not consider the vital idealistic dimension of nationalism. Thus Sombart considers all the talk among Germany's enemies of the defence of 'Western European civilisation' to be illogical since there is indeed no common 'Western European' culture when there is not even any compatibility between the cultures of the two close 'cousins', the Germans and the English.[15] In fact, the entire metaphysical significance of the First World War is the need to defend the idealistic worldview of Germany against the petty mercantile world of the English trader.

It is in this context that Sombart highlights the need for his German readers to consider themselves 'chosen' for a higher human mission, such as that which impelled the ancient Greeks among the barbarians and the Jews among the polytheists. It is, however, not certain that, apart from the later Spartans, the ancient Greeks

---

15 Sombart and the other German nationalists are clearly problematic thinkers for European nationalists like Jean Thiriart (1922–1992), who urged his followers to disregard all national differences in order to erect a pan-European political unit on the continent (see my editions of Jean Thiriart, *The Great Nation: Unitarian Europe — from Brest to Bucharest*, Melbourne: Manticore Press, 2018; *The Geopolitcal Unification of Europe, Russia and Central Asia*, Lewiston, NY: The Edwin Mellen Press, 2019; *Istanbul: The Geopolitical Capital of the United States of Europe, Russia and Central Asia*, Lewiston, NY: The Edwin Mellen Press, 2019; *Europe: An Empire of 400 Million*, London: Arktos, 2021).

cultivated the concept of heroic self-sacrifice in any nationalistic sense. For instance, the death of Achilles in Homer's *Iliad* results not from any willingness to continue the battle against the Trojans but rather from a desire to avenge the death of his friend Patroclus.[16] And, given Sombart's characterisation of the rational-realistic, anti-idealistic cast of the Jewish mind in *Die Juden und das Wirtschaftsleben* (1911), it is surprising that, at the end of the present work, he should point to the Jews as models for the modern Germans simply because they called themselves 'chosen people'. The rationalistic mentality of the Jews, manifested also in their unusual 'abstract idea of God', is not merely a contradiction of the idealism that he stresses throughout the work as the essential character of the German and the source of the heroic sense of self-sacrifice, it is also the means whereby the Jews developed their commercial prowess through the ages. It is clear, therefore, that the heroic spirit that Sombart evokes throughout this work is a more characteristically German, and especially Prussian, one that is related not to ancient Greek or Hebrew thought but, rather, to the idealistic philosophy developed by the Germans themselves in the late 18th and 19th centuries, starting with the writings of Kant and Wilhelm von Humboldt and Fichte's *Reden an die deutsche Nation* (1808).

In his *Deutscher Sozialismus*, written in 1934, Sombart reinforced the differences between the German and the Jewish ethos, as he had done in *Die Juden und das Wirtschaftsleben*, and did not focus on the English mentality so much. In *Händler und Helden*, on the other hand, Sombart neither discusses nor presents solutions to this problem. Here, his eloquent emphasis is on the statist ideal. The ideal of the state as the framework in which the citizen may seek to develop his personality to the fullest is characteristic of most of the German

---

16 See Homer, *Iliad*, IX, 410ff. In fact, it is the Trojan prince Hector who is a truly heroic warrior, as his moving farewell to his wife Andromache in *Iliad*, VI, 440ff. reveals.

thinkers of the 19th and early 20th centuries. In all of them, we note the stress on the state as representing the supraindividual dimension of man, and thus being tantamount to a collective 'Superman'. Of course, the idealist state is not the same as Nietzsche's 'Superman'. It is true that Sombart himself attempts in the present work to interpret Nietzsche's thought as idealistic, but this is contrary to Nietzsche's own repudiation of all idealism in favour of a new amoralist philosophy. As Nietzsche explained in *Ecce Homo*:

> Zarathustra created this most disastrous error, morality; consequently, he must also be the first to recognize it ... His doctrine, and his alone, has truthfulness as the highest virtue, that is, the opposite of the cowardice of the "idealist", who flees from reality ... Am I understood? — The self-overcoming of morality through truthfulness; the self-overcoming of the moralist into his opposite — into me — that is what the name of Zarathustra means in my mouth.[17]

Of course, it may be argued that the idealistic conception of the state included a Nietzschean element insofar as it sought to justify the expansionist, if not colonial, ambitions of the German state based on the 'higher' morality of the latter. This is indeed evident in Treitschke's glorification of war, which we have noted above, as well as in the conclusion of Sombart's *Händler und Helden*:

> We wish to be and remain a strong German nation and thus a strong state and thus also grow within the limits of the organic. And if it is necessary that we expand our territorial possession so that the greater national body may obtain space to develop itself we shall take as much land for ourselves as seems necessary. We shall also set foot where it seems important to us for strategic reasons to maintain our inviolable strength. We shall, therefore, if it benefits our position of power on earth, establish naval bases in Dover, Malta and the Suez. Nothing more. We do not wish to 'expand' at all. For we have more important things to do.

---

17   *Ecce Homo*, 'Warum ich ein Schicksal bin' (Why I Am a Destiny).

However, even if one does not agree with this expansionist dimension of German thought, it cannot be denied that Sombart's opposition of the German ethos to the English mercantilism retains a crucial significance for European political philosophy today — a hundred years after its original publication — since the British trader's worldview, which Sombart focused on as the principal opponent of the German one, not only defeated the latter in two world wars but continues to rule the world today, if not through the British colonial empire, still through the related American commercial one. And the philosophical and artistic sterility that Sombart had pointed to in British mercantilism ('No spiritual cultural value can grow out of trade. Not now and not ever') is in greater danger of debilitating the world now through the Atlanticist enterprise, which values 'comfort' and 'sports' far more than the British Empire did.

Life is not the highest of possessions.

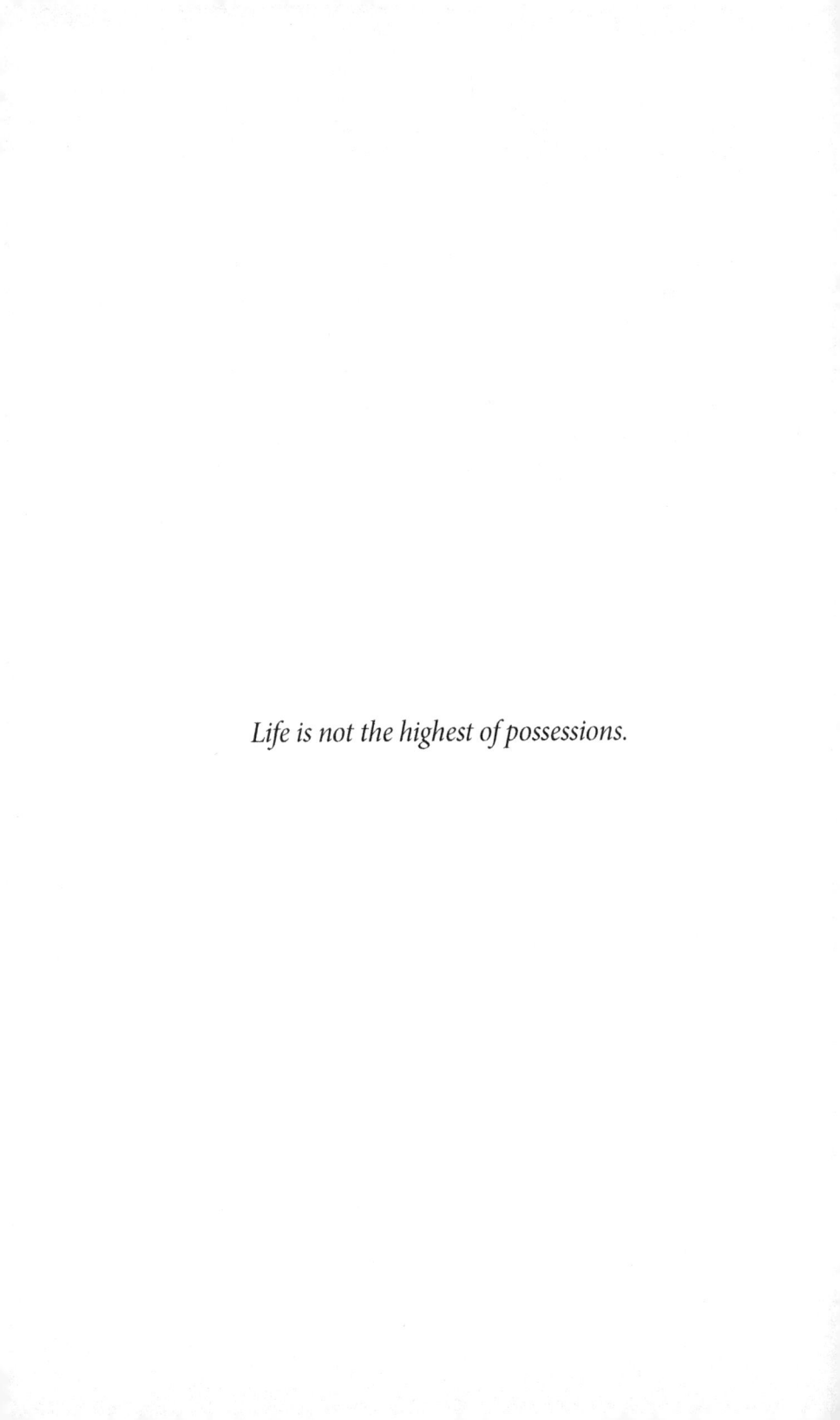

To you, young heroes,
    out there facing the enemy,

I DEDICATE THIS WORK, which also would like to take part in the battle that you now fight and that must continue in peacetime when you have returned home. Except that then it will be a battle of minds.

This work will show you the direction where the enemy of the German character is to be found in the future. But it especially wishes to tell you what you are fighting for.

A new, a German, life should begin after the war, and you should produce it. You who return home with a free and pure mind, and whose fresh youthful strength will break the thousand restrictions and prejudices and firmly held views that have burdened our nation so seriously up till now, you are our hope and our confidence.

Like a powerful ploughshare, the war draws its furrows through the wasteland of the German mind. It digs up the matted and kneaded turf and throws up the fertile soil from the depths of our souls once again to the wind and sun. Happy is the sower who may scatter his seeds on this steaming soil.

May the ideas that this work contains be part of those grains that fall on fertile ground, which rise and bear thousands of fruits.

Mittel-Schreiberhau,
in the seventh month of the war.
W.S.

INTRODUCTION

CHAPTER ONE

THE RELIGIOUS WAR

ALL GREAT WARS ARE RELIGIOUS WARS, so they were in the past, are in the present and will be in the future. Earlier they were that even in the consciousness of the warriors: whether Charlemagne fought against the Saxons, whether the 'Franks' set out for the liberation of the Holy Sepulchre, whether, later, the invading Turks were beaten back, whether the German emperors defended their empire against the Italian cities, whether Protestants and Catholics fought each other for supremacy in the Reformation age, the battle leaders were always aware that they were fighting for their faith and we, who attempt to recognise the world-historical significance of these wars in retrospect, understand that those feelings and thoughts of the warriors arose from a deep cause.

Even the Napoleonic Wars were not interpreted by the best of the age other than as religious wars. Thus the most recent biographer of Freiherr vom Stein[1] certainly judges the latter's conception of the Congress of Vienna[2] rightly when he says: to Freiherr vom Stein the

---
1 Heinrich Friedrich Karl Reichsfreiherr vom und zum Stein (1757–1831) was a noted Prussian statesman, who introduced social reforms based on Enlightenment doctrines that served to usher in the unification of Germany and the foundation of the German Empire. [All footnotes are by the translator.]
2 The Congress of Vienna (November 1814–June 1815) attempted to establish peace between the great powers on the continent after the defeat of Napoleonic France.

whole thing appeared not as a struggle for power but as a battle between good and evil.

In the age of nationalism and capitalism the deeper oppositions that are settled in the great world wars do not lie so much on the surface. Pure struggle for power or economic interests appear there, rather, as the sole reasons of the battles. And these could also be the motivating forces. But it would mean lingering on the surface if one did not wish to recognise behind these causes that are clear to the simplest minds, of the wars of our age and especially of the holy war that Germany now fights against a world of enemies, the deeper oppositions that exist in the war and that are once again religious oppositions or, as we are wont to say now, oppositions of worldview.

It is obvious that a number of different individual conflicts are being settled in the present world war. The wars that Russia conducts with Turkey for the possession of the Dardanelles, or France with Germany for Alsace-Lorraine or Austria-Hungary with Russia for supremacy in the Balkans, are incidental wars. The main war is another. Our enemies recognised this most clearly when they announced to the world: what is being fought over are 'Western European civilisation', 'the ideas of 1789', German 'militarism', German 'barbarism'. Here in fact, instinctively, the deepest opposition has been correctly expressed. I would like to express it only a little differently when I say: what stand opposed in battle are the trader and the hero, the worldviews of the trader and the hero and their corresponding cultures. Why I seek to highlight with these expressions a very profound, all-encompassing, opposition of worldview and experience of the world the following presentation should demonstrate.

Here I would just like to warn of a mistake, that I probably understand the terms trader and hero in a professional sense. That is naturally not the case, and cannot be if I use these expressions to indicate oppositions of worldview. For, the latter is not bound to certain professions with any natural necessity. It is a question, therefore, of a trader's or a heroic mentality, and it is perhaps possible that somebody who has been determined by fate to deal in pepper and raisins is (in mentality) a hero, whereas we see daily that a war minister is a 'trader' because he has the soul of a trader and not that of a warrior.

At first the individual man has a worldview, and so trader souls and heroic souls live next to one another in the same nation, the same city. But I predicate a war of nations related to worldviews and maintain, therefore, that traders and heroes stand in war against each other. Accordingly, we must be able to characterise entire nations too in one or the other sense. That occurs by attempting to grasp the soul of a nation, its spirit, its character. This 'national soul', this 'national spirit' — whether we conceive it metaphysically or purely empirically — is in any case a something whose existence cannot be denied; that has an independent existence beside, and above, all the individual members of a nation; that would remain even if all men died; that to a certain degree can maintain itself independently against living individual persons. This national soul speaks through the thousand characteristics of a nation (and will have to be recognised as different in every nation): through philosophy and art, through the state and politics, through mores and customs.

In this sense nations too can be distinguished as trader nations and heroic nations, and in this way do the trader's and the heroic worldviews stand in this war in a battle for supremacy. The bearers of these, however, the two nations that represent the oppositions in a characteristic manner, are the English and the Germans. And only as an English-German war does the world war of 1914 receive its deeper world-historical significance. But the important question for mankind that is to be decided now is not who should rule the seas; much more important, and encompassing all of mankind within itself, is the question: which spirit shows itself to be stronger: the trader's or the heroic?

For this reason we must make fully clear this opposition that spans all the depths and breadths of the world. And to help in this effort is the task of this work, in which I wish to describe plainly first the English and then the German mind in order to then evaluate them against each other and to present before the mind of the German reader — I do not write for any other — the incomparable superiority of the German mind so that he may be glad of his Germanness once again.

PART ONE

ENGLISH TRADERS

CHAPTER TWO

THE FEATURES OF THE ENGLISH MIND

THIS IS NOT THE PLACE to describe thoroughly the growth of the English mind, no matter how appealing the task may seem. I wish only to show in brief the components of which the English trader's spirit is composed and suggest what especially has encouraged its development.

The basis of all Englishness is indeed the immeasurable intellectual limitation of this people, their incapacity to raise themselves even a little distance beyond the tangible and the mundane 'reality'. Evidence of this: what is called 'philosophy' in England. Beginning with Francis Bacon, who, following the apt expression of Nietzsche, signifies an attack on the philosophical spirit in general,[1] to that man who was called throughout a generation just 'the philosopher': Herbert Spencer.

All these English philosophers are of a strangely uniform basic complexion: from Bacon to Spencer. And if anything typifies them in their innermost character, it is the remarkable circumstance that should especially be highlighted in every history of philosophy: that

---

1   See Nietzsche, *Beyond Good and Evil*, 252: 'They are not a philosophical race, these English. Bacon signifies an attack on the philosophical spirit in general, Hobbes, Hume and Locke a degradation and devaluation of the concept of a "philosopher" for over more than a century.'

they were indeed all rather good, partly excellent, national economists: Bacon wrote with good success about the colonial economy; Hobbes speaks always with an understanding outstanding for his age of economic problems; Locke's treatise on the monetary system[2] is as well-known as Hume's essays on trade, finance, interest, balance of trade, taxes, public credit, and similar subjects. Even Adam Smith, Jeremy Bentham and the two Mills are highly esteemed in England, whereas they are known to us only as national economists. And Herbert Spencer is of course not really a national economist, but may nevertheless be considered as the most influential 'philosopher' of our age.

That this tendency to economic problems, and this understanding of economic correlations that we find in almost all professional English 'philosophers', was no coincidence is shown by the fundamental orientation common to all of them.

Typical of the conception of the English thinkers is the discussion that Hebert Spencer once had with his deeper, but for that reason now not so famous, fellow countryman Matthew Arnold, who had opined that England was a country poor in ideas. To which Spencer replied in all seriousness that it was not so, since indeed England had in the last years 1. provided Amsterdam with water, 2. carried out the canalisation of Naples and 3. the Continental Gas Co. had provided all countries with gas. Indeed, Spencer continues literally, it is an incontestable fact that 'the headquarters of the mind, Berlin itself, must wait for this company to deliver light to it.' 'Should one not say therefore that more belief in ideas is proven among the English than among Germans?' And the one who speaks in this way is not an engineer of the Continental Gas Co. but an English 'philosopher': the philosopher of the modern age!

In this conception of the significance and value of ideas of the 'philosopher' Spencer there appears, besides, another characteristic of the English mind that has been of great importance for its development

---

2   *Some Considerations of the Consequences of the Lowering of Interest, and the Raising the Value of Money*, 1691.

into a trader's mind: the orientation of all English thought to practical goals. We find this characteristic strongly delineated already in the 'philosopher' of the age of Shakespeare, Francis Bacon, who called Greek philosophy a 'childish science' and 'professorial wisdom' since it was fruitful in words and unfruitful in works. He meant: the results and discoveries are, as it were, the guarantors that vouch for the truth of philosophy. 'The true and lawful goal of the sciences is none other than this: that human life be enriched with new discoveries and powers.'[3] 'The introduction of famous discoveries appears to hold by far the first place among human actions.'[4] Thus spoke Bacon, the founder of English 'philosophy'. To this day nothing has changed in this view.

This mundane way of thought then corresponds — apparently naturally — to a marked tendency to physical comfort, to material well-being, to 'comfort'. For we can trace back even this trait of the English character to earlier centuries. It already struck travellers in the 16th century as a characteristic of the English. A Venetian who visited England in the 16th century and left behind a well-known travel account narrates this to us of the English: 'when war rages most violently, they try to eat well and to have every other comfort (*vogliono cercare di ben mangare et ogn' altra loro commodità*)'; the same judgement is passed by Levinus Lemnius[5] in his travel account of 1560; the same by Pierre de Blois[6]. Indeed, a Dutchman (the historian Emanuel van Meteren, who lived from 1558 to 1612)[7] goes so far in his judgement as to consider the English as lazy, indolent; they lived comfortably, '*een*

---

3   Francis Bacon, *Novum Organum* (1620) (English translation, *The New Organon*, tr. James Spedding, Robert Leslie Ellis, and Douglas Denon Heath, Boston, 1863), LXXXI.

4   Ibid., CXXIX.

5   Lievin Lemmens (1505–1568) was a Dutch physician, who travelled in England and included a section called 'Notes on England' in his 1560 work *De habitu et constitutione corporis* (translated into English as *The Touchstone of Complexions*, 1576).

6   Pierre de Blois (ca. 1135–ca. 1203) was a French diplomat, who moved to England around 1173 and served as secretary to Henry II.

7   Emanuel van Meteren (1535–1612) was a Flemish historian, who worked as Consul for the Dutch merchants in London in 1581.

ledich leven leyende', like the Spanish (!): the hard, strenuous jobs they let foreigners take care of.

On the other hand, all observers already at that time think it necessary to notice a pronounced acquisitiveness among the English. It is especially interesting that this characteristic struck even the Venetian: '*tutti divengono cupidissimi del guadagno*'. All strive eagerly for money. One cannot inflict any injustice on the English people that cannot be compensated with money (*non è possibile fare tanta ingiuria alli inglesi plebei, la quale non si acconci con il denaro*). They are so eager in their trading businesses that they do not even shy away from usurious businesses (*sono tanto diligenti nella mercatura che non temano di fare contratti usurari*). Note that that was written by an Italian in 1500, that is, when England was still a good Catholic country.

Likewise characteristic of the English from ancient times is their obscurantism. It was no different in the 16th century than it is today. When they see a foreigner who looks handsome they say: pity that is not an Englishman, *dolore dicunt quod non sit homo Anglicus, vulgo Englishman*, recounts Paul Hentzler[8] in his travel account of 1598. The English are very conceited about themselves and their accomplishments; they do not think at all that there are other people than themselves or anything else in the world than England (*gli Inglesi sono molto amatori di se medesimi e d'ogni loro cosa; ne credono che si trovino altri huomini che loro; nè altro mondo che l'Inghilterra*), writes once again our Venetian source at the end of the 15th century.

It required only the initiation of a brilliant flowering of the capitalistic economy, especially a rapid flowering of trade, as was the case in England since the end of the 16th century (in 1591 the first ships sailed for India, the East India Trading Company was already founded in 1600) for the massive trader's worldview, which has already for a couple of centuries characterised the English nature as a whole, to be built upon these factors.

I understand by a trader's mentality that worldview that approaches life with the question: 'life, what can you give me?', that therefore

---

8   Paul Hentzler was a German who wrote about his travel to England.

views the entire existence of the individual on earth as a sum of trading businesses that every person concludes as advantageously as possible for himself with fate, or God (the religions are likewise stamped by the trader's mentality in this manner) or with his fellow men individually or as a whole (that is, with the state). The benefit for the life of every individual that should emerge from that is the greatest comfort possible, of which a supply of material goods suited for the beautification of life is a part. Within the scope of this view of life, a wide space is thus accorded to material values, and therewith that activity that occupies itself with the procurement of means to comfort, with material goods, that is, the economic and especially the trading activity, rises to respectability and esteem. The economic interests therefore acquire a predominance and gradually subordinate to themselves the other spheres of life. Once the representatives of the economy obtain the upper hand in a country they will then easily transfer the views of their professional life to all spheres of life, and the trader's view of the world will experience a considerable strengthening and consolidation, until the trader's worldview and practical commercialism finally combine into a unity that can no longer be divided, as is the case in present-day England.

That the process of the commercialisation of all of English culture has occurred so completely and thoroughly is connected once again to a series of events in the history of Great Britain, of which I wish to highlight only the most significant: I mean the infusion of all strata of the population with theoretical and practical commercialism, especially the complete commercialisation of the English nobility. Hardly one of the noble families of England living today is of feudal origin. Almost all arose from business. And then the noble families have entered into marriages for centuries with the trading citizenry so that there is generally in England not an estate that is removed from business life, since indeed the lower nobility — the gentry — is automatically formed and has acquired a capitalistic character to the degree that the capitalistic interests gained in importance. That the remaining population has become so fully commercialised is based first on the fact that, through the institution of the mercenary army, all warlike instincts were eradicated from the masses and that, as we see even today, all the elements of the population that have long resisted the commercialisation (the peasantry) have almost fully disappeared, so that there are in England, professionally, almost only men who are connected directly or indirectly to commerce.

Consequently, then, all the ruling circles of England, the English bureaucracy, are filled with the mercantile mentality. The superiority of England in the trade war being conducted now is traced back by a Hamburg businessman, the author of the work *Der englische Seeräuber* (The English Pirate), rightly to the circumstance 'that England possesses a line of bureaucrats that have emerged either directly from trading circles or at least from a trading milieu and come constantly in contact with the predominantly trading population'.

This standardisation of commercial interests, along with the natural superficiality of the English mind (common sense) then had the well-known effect that the English mind has today become a uniform one. Every foreign observer is struck today by the massiveness of the English national soul and its undifferentiated nature. The 'leaders' of the English nation are proud that they feel one with the man-in-the-street, that therefore there no longer exists any difference between the instincts and thoughts of the lowest and the highest. This condition naturally did not arise because the lower strata were raised very high; I am certain that they, the English worker, the English clerk, the English entrepreneur, stand intellectually far below the corresponding social circles in Germany. But, on the contrary, because the heights have for so long been degraded that they were brought to the same level with the depths. One may compare the intellectuality of a Grey[9] with that of a Bethmann-Hollweg.[10]

---

9   Sir Edward Grey (1862–1933) was a British liberal politician, who served as Foreign Secretary from 1905 to 1916. He was instrumental in Britain's declaring war on Germany in August 1914.

10 Theodor von Bethmann-Hollweg (1856–1921) was a Prussian politician, who served as Chancellor of the German Empire from 1909 to 1917.

CHAPTER THREE

ENGLISH SCIENCE

It would once again be an interesting task to provide the evidence of how all scientific thought in England, if it is not born of a commercial spirit, is still borne by and infused with it. That is true even of the natural sciences, at least those that have to do with the life-processes in nature. It has rightly been demonstrated by professionals recently that the English biology and evolutionary doctrine that has become so famous is basically nothing else but the transference of liberal-bourgeois views to the life-processes of nature. How much more must the humanities, whose source of knowledge is one's own inner life, be infused with this general English national mentality! Not to mention philosophy, which I have already referred to!

But I shall, in accordance with the goal set in this work, content myself with showing how the trader's mentality is impressed in those sciences that are related to the state and society, among which one can count ethics because it is oriented in a completely utilitarian way, and is thus necessarily sociologically based.

But one cannot wish to deny that there is a marked ethics and social doctrine that, from Hobbes and Locke to John Stuart Mill and Herbert Spencer, in spite of differences in viewpoint in details, agrees in its fundamental conception. And one will not be able to disprove it by pointing to individual exceptional cases. Already the fact that the latter as such stand out clearly from the traditional English doctrine proves that there is a rule. In addition, they can be explained easily by quite special circumstances. One cannot consider Carlyle generally as an English mind since from early on he absorbed only German intellectual food (of which, as many think, his English stomach became sick). But Edmund Burke, to name the perhaps most significant social philosopher, who, to be sure, wrote in English and who, as one knows, exercised a sustained influence on many German thinkers of his time, that is among the Romantics, was an Irishman — thus one can say anti-English. As indeed, fortunately, almost always where we meet an author writing in English with wit and profundity it can be determined that he is of Irish blood. That is true especially of the poets. I think of cases like Yorick Sterne,[1] of whom Goethe said that he was the 'finest mind', who influenced Ruskin, Oscar Wilde and Bernard Shaw, who, no matter how one may judge them otherwise, were not superficial and plain as is characteristic of the English type.

Indeed, superficial and plain is all genuinely English ethics, superficial and plain everything that Englishmen have written on the state. And every thought is born of a trader's mentality.

All the scientific ethics of England, like all the thought of a trader, starts from the small, petty life that Mr. X and Y lead. Or, to use a Fichtean expression: the object of their normative thought is, just as that of their causal thought, not life in itself but 'this or that life'. Thus, basically: the dead. For, our individual life is as much dying and death as life. For which reason Fichte could fully rightly characterise 'foreign philosophy' as 'devoted to death'. This individual little man then concludes a pact, so the utilitariarian-eudaimonistic ethics maintains, with life according to which he promises a series of performances but only in view of an advantageous reciprocation (no matter whether here or above). The most infamous saying that a tradesman's soul could ever utter: deal 'well' 'so that you may prosper and live long on

---

[1] Laurence Sterne (1713–1768) was an Irish novelist, who sometimes used the pseudonym 'Yorick'.

earth' has become the motto of all the doctrines of the English ethics. 'Happiness' is the highest goal of human ambition. 'The greatest happiness of the greatest number',[2] thus did Jeremy Bentham express in words for all time this rotten 'ideal'. In what this 'happiness' of the individual consists, for the procurement of which the gigantic, complicated apparatus of the whole world should be set in motion, the various ethicists have determined differently, each according to his personal predisposition. But even here a sort of average opinion can be noticed: 'happiness' is comfort with respectability: apple-pie and Sunday service, peaceableness and football, money-making and leisure for some hobby. The 'virtues' that one should cultivate are those that are guaranteed by a peaceful cohabitation of traders. I call them the negative virtues because they all amount to not doing what we instinctively perhaps would gladly do: temperance, frugality, industry, honesty, austerity in all things, humility, patience, etc. One sees what Herbert Spencer esteems as the 'truly human feelings' (*Principles of Sociology*, Art. 574): respect of the property of others, fastidious observance of marriage contracts, respect for the individuality of others, the sense of independence.

From these degradations of the ethics of social reciprocity are born also the trader's conceptions of 'justice' and 'freedom'. The formula of justice in Spencer (whom we can always cite in cases of doubt as the author who expresses the baseness of English thought best as a representative of it): 'Every man is free to do that which he wills, provided he infringes not the equal freedom of any other man' (*Principles of Ethics*, II, Art. 272). Freedom is therefore equated with caprice (positively) and independence (negatively) and, indeed, basically through the conclusion of daily trade businesses with which 'the higher man',

---

2 The phrase 'The greatest good for the greatest number' was originally coined by the Scottish Enlightenment thinker Frances Hutcheson (1694-1746) in his *Inquiry Concerning Moral Good and Evil* (1725), and later adapted by Jeremy Bentham (1748-1832), the English utilitarian, in *A Fragment on Government* (1776).

in the opinion of this Englishman, increasingly exclusively fills his life. These moral postulates of freedom=caprice+independence were generally developed first through endless trading and bargaining, for which reason they are established and represented only in 'advanced' countries like England. The following sentence of the classic representative of the pure shopkeeper philosophy speaks volumes:

> Daily exchange of services under agreement, involving at once the maintenance of personal claims and respect for the claims of others, has fostered a normal self-assertion and consequent resistance to unauthorized power. The facts that the word "independence," in its modern sense, was not in use among us before the middle of the last century, and that on the continent independence is less markedly displayed, suggest the connexion between this trait and a developing industrialism.[3]

What does the Englishman know of freedom!

Herbert Spencer, whom I cite not only as the most recent and most authoritative 'moral philosopher', is therefore especially interesting as a type because he has fused the specifically English, that is, superficial, ethics with the specifically English, that is, superficial, evolutionary theory into a unity. He has achieved the stunt of proving that the commercialisation or, as he calls it, industrialisation, of mankind is part of the plan of the world. What English traders, what English 'respectability', have accomplished in the stultification and proletarianisation of culture and the human mind is the consequence of a 'natural' development (against which opinion nothing, with certain reservations, might be objected). But now comes the shamelessness: this flattening and atrophying is the morally higher because it is the 'natural' (one does not need to go closer here into the grotesque *salti mortali*[4] of logic with the help of which the 'natural' is transformed into the 'moral'). The survivor is the stronger (in the sense of the theory of the fittest); the stronger, the 'fit' person, is the morally higher one, the best

---

3 *Principles of Sociology*, Art. 574.
4 fatal leaps.

individuals, 'individuals best adapted for life in the industrial state' (*Principles of Sociology*, Art. 567); the 'industrial type of society' is the 'higher moral' condition.⁵

⁂

Even the state cannot be imagined by the trader other than in the image of a gigantic trading business that includes everything in itself. The 'contract theory' of political doctrine was basically born out of the true trader's mentality which was already alive at the time of late antiquity when this thought was conceived and which began to conquer Europe when the 'contract theory' celebrated its resurrection. It was seized upon eagerly in all trading countries by the 'statist philosophers' (Hugo Grotius!⁶) and attained sole rule in English politics from Hobbes on. Herbert Spencer goes beyond them to the extent that he allows the state to at least arise 'organically' (in the biological sense) even if the ideas of this emergence are totally those of the London man of the financial city: thus when he traces back the beginning of political life to the differentiation of the members of a community into three groups that are nothing but the chairman, board of directors, general meeting of a stock company; he himself points in Art. 470 of his *Principles of Sociology* to this analogy; or when he makes the English power of the purse a primordial institution of mankind (Arts. 500ff); and insofar as he supposes an earlier epoch of political history without contractual relations in which a naturally arisen 'status' ruled but only to assert the contract theory so much more strongly. That is, according to Spencer, those times of imperfect social formation were followed, through a 'natural development', by a period which he designates, in contrast to the first 'militant' society, as the 'industrial', and

---

5   Note to *Principles of Sociology*, Ch. XVIII.
6   Hugo Grotius (1583–1645) was a Dutch diplomat and lawyer, whose writings contributed to the development of international law between states.

the latter begins 'with the establishment of contract as the universal relation under which efforts are combined for mutual advantage'.[7]

The position of the individual to the state is now consciously the position of the trader calculating his advantage:

> 'Each citizen wants to live, and to live as fully as his surroundings permit.'
>
> The state has 'to maintain the conditions under which each may gain the fullest life compatible with the fullest lives of fellow citizens'.[8]

The individual has with regard to the state only 'rights', basically only the rights to carry on free trade. Spencer enumerates in his *Principles of Ethics* the following 'human rights' (=civic rights):

1. The right to physical integrity. 'The right to life has acquired the leading place in thought',[9] life always conceived in the trivial sense designated above.

2. The rights to free motion and locomotion

3. The rights to the uses of natural media (light, air, the earth's surface)

4. The right of property

5. The right of intellectual property

6. The rights of gift and bequest

7. The rights of free exchange and free contract

8. The right of free industry

9. The right of free belief and worship

10. The rights of free speech and publication[10]

---

7   *Principles of Sociology*, Art. 571.
8   *Principles of Ethics*, I, Art. 361.
9   Ibid., Art. 285.
10 *Principles of Ethics*, Part IV, 'Contents'.

It is well-known how this superficial trader's conception of the state finally leads to that which can be called fear of the state. The less state the better—that is the melody that all political theorists since Locke sing. The ideal to which the 'industrial society' moves is total statelessness. And to let the 'philosopher' speak again:

> The remaining end to be achieved by public action is to keep private actions within due bounds ... (Art. 563)
>
> Internal protection must become the cardinal function of the state (Art. 564)
>
> Nearly all public organizations save that for administering justice, necessarily disappear; since they have the common character that they either aggress on the citizen by dictating his actions, or by taking from him more property than is needful for protecting him, or by both. (Art. 569)

This English conception of the state has been ineradicably impressed in our minds by the term used by Ferdinand Lassalle, who called it a 'nightwatchman's idea':

> a nightwatchman's idea because it can think of the state itself only in the image of a nightwatchman, whose entire function consists in preventing robbery and burglary.[11]

On another occasion he called the Manchester men[12]

> modern barbarians who hate the state, not this or that particular state but the state in general and who, as they have repeatedly clearly admitted,

---

11 Ferdinand Lassalle, Talk 'Über den besonderen Zusammenhang der gegenwärtigen Geschichtsperiode mit der Idee des Arbeiterstandes', April 1862, in Ferdinand Lassalle, *Reden und Schriften*, Bremen: Europäischer Hochschulverlag, 2010, p. 152.

12 The principal champions of liberal free-trade economics based in the textile manufacturing city of Manchester were Richard Cobden (1804–1865) and John Bright (1811–1889), who founded the Anti-Corn Law League in order to repeal the protectionist Corn Laws of 1815–1846. Free-trade economists were followers of the doctrines of the Scottish Enlightenment thinker Adam Smith (1723–1790).

would like most to abolish the state, sell the judiciary and the police to the one asking for the lowest price and would like to conduct war through stock companies ...'[13]

Lassalle followed here his great teacher Fichte, who had already expressed his view of this trader's theory of the state in a similar way: 'This view of the state is indeed quite general in the schools of wisdom...', says Fichte. 'It manifests itself in the eagerness for freedom, that is, the lawlessness of acquisition ... in the opinion that the state would entirely disappear if there were no more robbers because everything else lies outside its jurisdiction.'[14] According to this view 'the proprietors possess the state as a lord possesses a servant.' 'The state, they maintain, is a necessary evil because it costs money; but one must make every evil as small as possible.'

It has been maintained that social Manchesterism is a worldview of the bourgeoisie, that it is therefore conditioned by the characteristics of a class or socially. No less than Ferdinand Lassalle posited this thought at the base of all his works and speeches. 'Thence (in order to better exploit the worker, he means) the hatred of our liberal bourgeoisie for the state, not for a specific state but for the concept of the state in general, which they would most like to abolish entirely and let it degenerate into that of the bourgeois society, that is infuse it totally with free competition ... Thence especially the concentrated hatred of the bourgeoisie for every strong state, however it may be organised and constituted ...'[15] That was a mistake of Lassalle's. It may be admitted that the class interests of the bourgeoisie approach most closely the anti-statist philosophy; but the two do not coincide at all. There are also bourgeois with a pronounced state feeling. There are theories

---

13 Lassalle, *Die indirekte Steuer und die Lage der arbeitenden Klassen, Eine Vertheidigungsrede*, Zürich: Meyer und Zeller, 1863, p. 136.
14 Johann Gottlieb Fichte, *Die Staatslehre*, Zweiter Abschnitt: 'Über den Begiff des wahrhaften Krieges', 1813.
15 Ferdinand Lassalle, *Die Philosophie Fichtes und die Bedeutung des deutschen Volksgeistes* (Festrede, Mai 1862), Berlin, 1877, p. 170.

of the state that were sketched fully independently of any class interests. On the other hand, there are also anti-capitalistic efforts aplenty that are born of the eudaimonistic-individualistic-Manchester spirit. Indeed, there is not a single English orientation of socialism or of the workers' movement that is not eudaimonistically-individualistically orientated, that is, that does not arrive at the community starting from the rights of the individual and does not have the greatest happiness of the greatest number as its goal.

Thomas More, who had indeed nourished his mind on Plato's ideas and from whom most of all one would expect a different conception, however lets his Utopians find their contentment in the most superficial, English middle-class happiness.

> 'the soule is ... by the bountiful goodnes of God ordeined to felicitie.'[16]
>
> '[The Utopians] are enclyned to the opinion of them, which defende and holde pleasure, wherein they determine either all or the chiefyste parte of mans felicitye to reste.'
>
> Not in every pleasure, adds the wise chancellor, but only in the 'respectable' [English 'respectability' demands that].

And that is how it has remained. One may consider any of the great 'socialists', whether Godwin[17] or Thompson[18] or Owen;[19] no matter how different they may otherwise be from each other, they remain the same in their theoretical bases as in their practical ideals: society is an aggregate of individuals, its goal is to promote the greatest happiness

---

16 All English translations of More are from *The Utopia of Sir Thomas More*, tr. Ralph Robinson (1556), ed. George Sampson, London: G. Bell and Sons, 1914.

17 William Godwin (1756–1836) was an English anti-statist 'Jacobin' thinker, whose chief work was *An Inquiry Concerning Political Justice*, 1793.

18 William Thompson (1775–1833) was an Irish socialist political thinker, who published a work entitled *An Inquiry into the Principles of the Distribution of Wealth* in 1824.

19 Robert Owen (1771–1858) was a Welsh socialist thinker, who advocated the establishment of collective cooperative communities.

of the greatest number. And none of the English workers' leaders, whether revolutionary or reformatory, has ever conceived a different idea than this. (Carlyle is always a completely un-English unique case). No — the basic views of the state and society are not socially but nationally conditioned. And the individualistic-eudaimonistic social philosophy is originally and in the deepest sense an emanation of the English mind (to what extent, and in what — noticeably — special form, also of the French mind is not to be discussed here).

❧

The theoretical attitude of the trader to war is produced automatically from his fundamental views: his ideal must be 'eternal' peace. He may start from the narrower interests of the economy, to which indeed he concedes such a wide space in his value system, or he may choose the general trader's worldview as the guideline for his judgement.

That the international investment and trade, especially the large overseas trade (in its present-day civilised forms, it may be noted!), required peace for its flourishing can be perceived by any child. When it has really become important that bacon and cotton goods are transported undamaged from one place on earth to another, how should one not consider every war disturbance as irreconcilable with the advancements of civilisation? Indeed, since the progressive commercialisation of mankind is considered part of the development of higher life-forms, the moral demand of eternal peace is indeed an obvious consequence.

But, even without the direct consideration of the unhindered course of the economic process, the general trader's worldview must lead to the rejection of war.

Since the representatives of this view have never hoped for anything further from life than 'the continuation of the custom of living in tolerable conditions', there is indeed no visible reason why one should not live peacefully and amicably on earth, if it be possible anywhere. Comfort is not heightened by a war in any way. And especially when the greatest happiness of the greatest number is the goal and purpose of life, and especially of political life: how can the sacrifice of individual men in war be justified? Why, every person who is asked to expose himself to foreign bullets will rightly ask: should I die so that others may partake of the happiness to which I have no smaller claim than they?

The logic of the trader thus leads necessarily, in the first place, to the rejection of every war and secondly: insofar as a war, which naturally can only be a 'defensive war', cannot be avoided, then only for the promotion of the mercenary army, which is indeed based on the principle that soldiering, like any other trade, is conducted for the sake of profit. If one maintains the 'voluntariness' of the enlistment, one has followed the principles of the trader's morality conscientiously.

That, then, has also been the standpoint of all theorists of the state in England: war is a necessary evil, if it must indeed be carried out, then as far as possible 'by others' and — it may be added — with all the chicaneries of commercialist technique. That is what they have taught from Thomas More down to, once again, our Herbert Spencer.

Thomas More merits special consideration. He wrote his *Utopia* (published 1516) in an age when the English nation was in no way fully commercialised, in an age in which the foreigners who came to England highlighted the warlike capacities of the English even panegyrically. '*Sono molto reputati nell'arme*' writes our source, the Venetian author of the *Relatione,* in 1500. Not surprising. The generation that had fought the war between York and Lancaster still lived and its oldest members had experienced even the wars with France. To be sure, even at that time a strong turn towards trade seems to have entered. Did the warlike spirit of the people bleed to death in the battles of the Civil War? And was the work of the chancellor More written from a longing for peace, which is a cry of the English trader's mind for redemption from the evil of war, and from which (in spite, or because, of its anti-capitalistic tendency) the entire trading-oriented political philosophy of the later English may be read?

What More says on the attitude of the Utopians to war is so interesting because his programme includes in every point (as I shall show later) what was realised by the English in the following centuries: a sufficient proof how native these views that More represents are to the trader's way of thinking and feeling.

Here are a couple of passages from *Utopia* which prove what has been said:

> Warre or battel as a thing very beastly, and yet to no kinde of beastes in so muche use as to man, they do detest and abhorre. And contrarie to the custome almooste of all other nations, they counte nothynge so much against glorie, as glory gotten in warre.' Nevertheless 'they do daylie practise and exercise themselves in the discipline of warre' [the kernel of sportism!]

> they never go to battell, but either in the defence of their owne countrey or to drive, out of their frendes lande the enemies that have invaded it, or by their power to deliver from the yocke and bondage of tirannye some people, that be therewith oppressed, Which thing they do of meere pitie and compassion [the kernel of English cant!]

> They be not only sory, but also ashamed to atchieve the victorie with bloudshed, counting it greate folie to bie precious wares to dere. They rejoyse and bought avaunt themselves if they vanquishe and oppresse their enemies by craft and deceite.

> immediatlye after that warre is ones solemnelie denounced, they procure many proclamations signed with their owne commen seale to be set up privilie at one time in their enemies lande, in places moste frequented. In these proclamations they promise greate rewardes to hym that will kill their enemies prince, and some what lesse giftes, but them verye greate also, for everye heade of them, whose names be in the saide proclamations conteyned.' etc. 'in rewardes they kepe no measure.'

> This custome of byinge and sellyinge adversaryes among other people is dysallowed, as a cruel acte of a basse and a cowardyshe mynde. But they in this behalfe thinke themselves muche prayse worthy ...

> Yf by none of these meanes the matter goo forwarde as they woulde have it, then they procure occasyons of debate, and dissention to be spredde amonge theire enemies.

CHAPTER THREE. ENGLISH SCIENCE

Yf this waye prevayle not, then they reyse up the people that be nexte neygheboures and borderers to theire enemyes, and them they sette in theire neckes under the coloure of some olde tytle of ryghte, such as kynges doo never lacke. To them they promysse theire helpe and ayde in theire warre. And as for moneye they gyve them abundaunce. But of theire owne cytyzeins they sende to them fewe or none.

But their gold and silver, bycause they kepe it all for thys only purpose, they laye it owte frankly and frely besydes theire ryches, whyche they kepe at home, thei have also an infinite treasure abrode, by reason that (as I sayde before) manye nations be in their debte

The Utopians employ by preference the war leaders of the Zapoletes, a 'hideous, savage and fyerce' people living 500 miles east of Utopia 'dwellynge in wild woodes and high mountaines, where they were bredde and brought up' [thereby could be meant the Germans or the Swiss].

This people fighteth for the Utopians agaynste all nations, bycause they geve them greatter wayges, then annye other nation wyll.

Nor the Utopianes passe not how many of them they bring to destruction.

Next unto thies they use the soldiours of them for whom they fighte. And then the helpe of their other frendes. And laste of all [!], they joyne to theire oune citizens ...

They chuese soldyours out of every citye those whych putte furthe themselffes wyllyngelye. For they thruste no man forthe into warre agaynste his wyll ...

For as they make all the meanes and shyftes that maye be to kepe themselfes from the necessitye of fyghtinge, or that they may dispatche the battell by their hiered soldyours: so when there is no remedy, but that they must neades fight themselfes, then they do as corragiously fall to it, as before, whyles they myght, they did wiselye avoyde and refuse it ...

One never knows, in the case of More, where his seriousness ends and where his sarcasm starts. So this ideal conduct of war can mean as well a mockery of the traders that the great chancellor saw rising among his countrymen and gaining power at that time. With what feelings would he experience the war of 1914 on seeing his 'Utopians' carry out the programme outlined four hundred years earlier! But I shall speak about the trading practice in the appropriate context later. Here, alongside the view of the chronologically first of the English social philosophers, the conception of the significance and character of war of the last may be described in a few words.

War, says Herbert Spencer, earlier bestowed blessings. Today we do not need it any more; today it is superfluous; today trade and industry conduct everything far better. Today war has as its consequence only social disadvantages. 'With the repression of militant activities and the decay of militant organisations will come amelioration of political institutions as of all other institutions. Without them no such ameliorations are permanently possible.' (*Principles of Sociology*, Art. 582)

In Spencer's view only a 'defensive war' is justified because (note well!) the whole is maintained through the sacrifice of a smaller or greater number of individuals. But even a 'defensive war' has a significance only if an effective defence has a prospect of success. 'For it would seem to be an implication that where the invading force is overwhelming, such sacrifice of individuals is not justified.' [!] (*Principles of Ethics*, II, Art. 288). Withdrawal of the English troops from besieged Antwerp! I shall speak further about that.

> Such contingent loss of life and partial loss of liberty as are entailed on soldiers, and such deductions from their earnings as other citizens have to contribute to support soldiers, are felt by each to be justified as instrumental to the supreme end of enabling him to carry on his activities and to retain the reward for them — sacrifice of a part to ensure the remainder.[20] [!]

Nice people, our 'cousins'!

---

20 *Principles of Ethics*, II, Art. 358.

CHAPTER FOUR

THE ENGLISH STATE AND ENGLISH CULTURE

There is nothing like the English state in history. Perhaps the trading countries of antiquity, those of the Phoenicians and Carthaginians, represented on a small scale something similar. But there has never yet been a 'world empire' born of a purely mercantile spirit. The characteristic of the English state is indeed based on the fact that it contains nothing of all that one had until then sensibly considered of the state, that is, that it is an organically ordered community of men joined together into a cultural and civilisatory unity to which perhaps 'colonies' could belong as external outworks corresponding to its size. Everything that we have learnt up to now of great states is grown organically and from inner vital impulses. The English world empire, however, is like investment capital that is mechanically ordered piece by piece, one next to the other: the individual components are 'accumulated' and are connected loosely to one another and with the mother country. What does it mean that India, a country with 300 million people, 'belongs' to Great Britain? This belonging has a meaning only if one tries to understand the entire British world empire in a commercialistic spirit, that is, tries to comprehend it not as a state but as a big emporium in which the mother country represents the headquarters, where the central treasury and central bookkeeping are, whereas the colonies are the subsidiaries.

How fully inorganically England has been formed can be learnt by a glance at the statistics. Clearly a state whose inhabitants do not belong mostly, I would almost say in most part, to agriculture is a malformation. By now the percentage of people occupied in agriculture (and the very considerable fisheries!) has sunk to 8 (!) percent. Compared to this twelfth is an entire fourth of professional traders (almost 25% of the inhabitants of England are occupied in trade and commerce) and almost half of the inhabitants of England (45%) are engaged in industry. A state ordered professionally in such a way is a caricature, is no longer a living unity but only a trading station. The 'colonies' are pump stations that have the sole purpose of channelling surpluses either directly or (mostly) indirectly to the mother country. One can follow that clearly in individual cases, how only this mercantile exploitation of a territory leads to its inclusion in the colonial property or how the investment in a region makes it appear 'ripe' for annexation. I am thinking of Egypt, Angola, Mesopotamia.

According to the latest estimates of the Manchester Social Society, England has invested 74.7 billion marks abroad, of which 35.9 in the colonies. But if one subtracts from these investments the fixed interest loans that are naturally given particularly to independent foreign states, certainly the greatest part of the actual investment is made in the colonies. The mother country essentially serves to lead this gigantic 'English world empire' enterprise and to calculate the revenues and expenses. That is the massive Leviathan that Hobbes had foreseen in his mind when he sketched his ideal picture of a state, of which he said that its power consists in the wealth of the individual citizens (!): *divitiae singularium hominum sunt pro robore.*[1]

---

[1] Thomas Hobbes, 'Introductio', in the Latin translation (1668) of *Leviathan* (1651). The English original is: 'the wealth and riches of all the particular members are the strength [of the commonwealth, or Leviathan]'.

If we wish, following the process of Hobbes, to imagine the English state in the image of an organism, Great Britain appears like one of those giant polyps that consists only of tentacles and an enormous digestive apparatus, whereas all other organs, the head, heart, and whatever else is of significance in differentiated organisms, have atrophied.

Just as the English state structure was born of a commercialistic spirit, all the methods of state policy are naturally also derived from the sphere of mercantile thoughts and ideas. It is uncommonly instructive to observe how through English politics that instrument of power comes to the forefront and is made the actual instrument of political transactions which is produced directly from the trading spirit: the contract.

If one surveys the overseas history of England, especially also its economic and particularly its trade history, it can be ascertained that England's greatness was chiefly brought about by its outstanding skill in concluding contracts. If one wishes to explain the enormous upsurge that the English economy experienced in the 18th century, one must especially consider that, at the beginning of the century, two contracts were concluded on account of which England succeeded in drawing to itself before all other nations the flow of precious metals from the Spanish and Portuguese colonies, whose influx first made possible for it all the other large trade with Europe and the East. The two contracts that I have in mind are the Methuen Treaty (1703)[2] and the Asiento (1713).[3]

---

2   The Methuen Treaty, signed between England and Portugal in December 1703, encouraged the import of Portuguese wine by England but had a deleterious effect on the development of Portuguese industry.

3   In 1713 the British were granted an *asiento*, or monopoly on a trade route or product, as part of the treaties constituting the Peace of Utrecht that ended the War of the Spanish Succession. The Peace of Utrecht established Britain as the leading European maritime and commercial power.

That, along with skilled contract drafting, all the methods of betrayal, breach of contract, cheating, theft, robbery went hand in hand is known to every student of English history. The 'moral insanity' of this nation is, in no little part, the secret of its power. But what interests us here is not the machinations of the cheating trader, whom England had at all times favoured, but those of the trader as such. For what we would like to recognise is indeed the birth of the whole of England from the spirit of the trader.

Here we must remember that, even in 'higher' politics, the skilled application of the contract has helped the nation to its success. For what basically was it through which India was 'conquered' and held in the empire? The commercially skilled exploitation of the thousand oppositions that fill India: between Mohammedans and Hindus, between the individual Nawabs and the Subahs[4] that separated themselves from the Great Mogul and sought to make themselves independent. We wish to always bear in mind that in the famous Battle of Plassey (23 June 1757),[5] through which India was conquered by England, 3,000 men fought on the English side of whom 900 (!) were Englishmen!

To conclude advantageous contracts (already the government of the 'Utopians' in More, who had understood the English national soul so deeply and thoroughly, considered this their chief task) and — what is directly related to it — to render hostile forces harmless by making them act against one another and thereby impeding their own endangerment: on that alone has England's attention been focused from time immemorial.

We know that the leading principle of English politics for some time has been: to maintain the 'balance of power' among the European states (just as the English policy in India is built on this principle). This

---

4 A province in the Mughal Empire.
5 The Battle of Plassey (Palashi, north of Calcutta) was fought by the British East India Company, led by Robert Clive, against the Nawab of Bengal and his French allies. Clive's victory resulted in the British acquisition of Bengal.

CHAPTER FOUR. THE ENGLISH STATE AND ENGLISH CULTURE

idea of 'balance of power' is born once again clearly from the trader's spirit; it is the image of the scales that the shopkeeper holds in his hand to weigh raisins and pepper. It saw the light of day in the Italian trading states of the Middle Ages and became perceptibly the principal idea of the English state. Even here the life-destroying character of the trader's mentality strikes us once again; it is a purely mechanical conception of everything political that wishes to hold 'forces' in 'balance'. One can 'weigh' only dead substances, but not living beings, which states in reality are. Already Adam Müller had poured out his scorn on the 'miserable image of the swaying scales ... As if international law were nothing but the result of political arithmetic'.[6]

But it is especially instructive now to observe how the trader conducts war: fully, we shall see, according to the programme of the trader theoreticians, a few of whom we have become acquainted with above. Since he knows no other interests than material ones, war can also have for him always only the significance that it protects or defends material interests. In England, thus, almost exclusively trading interests or the interests of capitalists abroad. In 1909, there appeared in the well-known monthly *The United Service Institution* the prize-winning work of a British naval officer. In it were such statements (which I cite here in the translation found in the work by Count Ernst zu Reventlow, *England, der Feind*):[7]

> We (Great Britain) do not go to war out of sentimental reasons. I doubt that we have ever done that. War is the result of trading activities; its goal is to force upon our enemies with the sword those economic conditions that we esteem necessary in order to produce for ourselves commercial advantages. We give all sorts of reasons for the war, but at the bottom of them all is commerce.

---

6   Adam Müller, *Die Elemente der Staatskunst*, Zehnte Vorlesung.
7   Ernst zu Reventlow, *England, der Feind*, Stuttgart, 1914.

Everybody who knows, even only superficially, the war history of England knows how truly this English naval officer has characterised the causes of all English wars. The 'England' commercial house was especially forced to the use of militant arms when it thought that it observed that a competing company was in the process of taking over its rank in the world market. Thence the wars against Spain in the 16th century, against Holland in the 17th, against France in the 18th century and now against us. But in every single case, the commercial reason for the wars that England has conducted or has had conducted for its sake, can be detected. I am thinking of the war that England declared in 1739 against Spain because an indemnity amount of the South Sea Company was not paid by Spain and wares of the South Sea Company had been withheld. I am thinking of the 'conquest' of India (in 1757) that Lord Clive undertook on behalf of the East India Trading Company to avenge, or defend, the clerks of the company attacked by the Nawab of Bengal. I am thinking of the participation of England in the Seven Years' War that is especially instructive: England supported Prussia because — in general — it had to see that the first trading and maritime power, France, of that time should be weakened, because it especially had an interest in seeing that France's supremacy in India be broken. But this occurred through the conquest and razing of Pondicherry (16 January 1761), while the conquest of Canada in 1760 had shaken France's position in the West. On 16 January 1761, thus, England's interest in Frederick's war was exhausted. Consequently it stopped its participation immediately! In December 1760, the Convention contract of England with Frederick II had been renewed with the great unanimity of the Parliament; in the following year, it was not renewed in spite of the sorrowful and humble letters of the great king to Pitt.

But I am also thinking of the wars of the 19th century that were directly conducted as trade or financial wars: of the Opium War (1840–42) against China, of the gold- and diamond-war against the Boers, of the war of 1914.

CHAPTER FOUR. THE ENGLISH STATE AND ENGLISH CULTURE

But just as the motivation of the war of these trader nations is a purely commercial one, the same that legally underlies every capitalistic enterprise, that is, to aim at the highest profits possible, the war itself too will be considered as nothing but a capitalistic enterprise and organised as such. The loftiest idea there then is: one does not conduct war oneself but lets war be conducted. Just as one buys means of production and workforce in a market for a cotton mill, so, following the principle of the mercenary army, cannons and soldiers. It is the old standpoint of the shopkeeper conducting a war, just as Carthage in antiquity and the banking states of Italy in the Middle Ages undertook it. Still better, and mercantilely more correctly thought out, is it to conduct not at all at one's own expense and danger but merely to participate in the enterprise with an investment; that was the procedure of the English in the 18th century when they flooded the European states with their subsidies. Unfortunately, business can no longer be conducted quite so comfortably nowadays. Businesses are generally harder to undertake today; that is indeed a general sign of our times, and even here the 'damned Germans' have made life sour for the poor Brits exactly as in the sales in the market.

Today a more artful procedure must be adopted to make foreign nations fight for England's trade interests; when one cannot simply issue an order to them as to subsidiaries or agencies of the mother company 'to provide' so many men (in this manner do they proceed with the colonial peoples, who naturally are foreigners for the English in England, and with vassal states like Egypt, Portugal), they must either enter into a partnership relationship, which is the right one between like-minded nations, or — where one must still reckon with decency and chivalry, as with the French — one must know how to exploit their weaknesses deftly to make them too participate in the enterprise.

If now the enterprise is set in motion, the watchful eye of the trader has to see that it will be conducted with the greatest profit possible and the least loss. Foreign troops cost England nothing; so they can be sacrificed at will; even foreign cities can be bombed (Antwerp,

Ostend with English cannons!). But one's own troops must be paid with cash; consequently they must be spared as much as possible. Especially one's own ships are perceptibly more expensive! What happened according to this mercantile principle, for example, in Antwerp cries out to the heavens. Without any thought of duty or loyalty or decency the English troops withdrew from the beleaguered fortress that they had to defend[8] at the right time to reach the ships in Ostend safe and sound. I am convinced that the thought did not occur, even for a moment, to the departmental heads who preside as ministers over the 'England Warehouse', Ltd. that that was an unmentionably dirty affair. If one were to reproach them for it, they would reply: but it was more practical to act in this way. And from their point of view, they are completely right. Indeed, we saw how their theorist, Herbert Spencer, preaches this utilitarian morality quite bluntly in his warehouse ethics.

But now, armed combat is for England only the incidental part of the war that it conducts against us; its participation with troops in the enterprise plays basically no role, and it does not send its fleet into battle, because it is too expensive. Its principal war is in the narrower sense a trade- and financial war such as real traders — and indeed unscrupulous ones, like the owners of two large warehouses of second rank — conduct between themselves. The most important war weapons that England itself employs are indeed direct commercial pressures and chicaneries that are especially determined to damage our material interests — the English business directorship hardly thinks of anything else: boycotting, patent theft, privateering, customer theft, bribery.

That there is privateering even today in which even the nations hostile to England, driven by necessity, must participate is due, as is

---

8   A reference to the Siege of Antwerp, when the fortified city of Antwerp was bombarded by the German forces from September 28, 1914. The city was defended by the Belgians and their British and French allies and, on their withdrawal, surrendered to the Germans on October 10.

CHAPTER FOUR. THE ENGLISH STATE AND ENGLISH CULTURE

well-known, to England alone. It reveals the inner character of its conduct of war that it considers this rotten form of war as basically its most important component, which it cannot 'do without', as it declares repeatedly at every international conference.

That the English government sends emissaries to all foreign markets during the war to lure away the customers from the German competition is well-known. How much they hope for this result, above all, from the war, that the German companies abroad are ruined, is proven by the following letter of a correspondent of the *Times* in Pahang (Malacca), which the paper published in its issue of 11 December 1914:

> This war is in the course of enriching a number of born traders. From the standpoint of a British industrialist, the longer the war lasts the better for British industry. Now we may feel the strain, in some years we will have the advantages. Every German company in the British colonies that has eaten deep into the entrails of British trade and commerce will then be ruined. I do not doubt that the generous, far-sighted, never failing British government is fully aware of this state of affairs. If we had possessed a great military force to rush into the battlefield and overcome Germany at the first onset, the results would not have been so wide-ranging. Slower, constant pressure, like the present, is all in all the best policy. (!)

The basest means of conducting war arisen from the lowest trader's instincts that England, as we know, has so masterfully employed during this war is that which has been called the 'journalistic encirclement' of Germany. With its money it has laid, or bought, all the cables in the world that it now unscrupulously exploits for the propagation of its false news; with its money it has bribed the telegraph offices, the newspapers and journals, the illustrators and press agents in neutral foreign countries, and in the allied states, to work for English interests. Always the trader from top to toe, this time also the sleazy trader. Never has a war been conducted so completely in a mercantile spirit, even not by England, because it perfects itself naturally every time in its trading technique — like this war. Often one really feels that a warehouse is fighting against us. Occasionally it is as if a businessman is playing a new trump card in the war with competitors when one reads the official English war reports: so, for example, when the arrival of the Indian troops in France is announced: 'An excellent article that beats everything before it has today reached me and is posted in the shop-window'. Advertisements, product promotion, devaluation of rivals: everything is part of the picture. Even the purely quantitative observation of the war arises from the same intellectual basis. How often already have we heard of the army of millions of Lord Kitchener, and that such and such a troop from Canada, India, Portugal will be arriving. Always figures and only figures. Once again quite logical considered from the standpoint of the capitalistic entrepreneur who sees in high turnovers the most certain sign of the flourishing of his business. With shameless frankness Churchill too (or was it Lloyd George?) declared: 'England will win because it has the last disposable million.' Here the capitalistic conception of things is no longer disguised; it is expressed bluntly: for us the war is a business like every other and, since we live in an age of capitalism, the business with the largest capital will triumph.

But the most disgusting thing that this war has brought to light is this: that it is considered by the English as a sort of sports. When the *Emden* was destroyed in a shelling of strongly superior strength,[9] the English press rejoiced openly. English trade had indeed been delivered from an inexorable enemy. But something incredible happened: the heroic Captain von Müller was praised to high heavens. If he went to London, so they said, he would be the most celebrated man. Why? Because he had accomplished heroic deeds in faithful fulfilment of duty to the Kaiser and the Reich? Oh no! But because he had accomplished such outstanding sportive actions! And when the imprisoned

---

9   The SMS *Emden* was a light cruiser of the Imperial German Navy that was attacked in November 1914 by the Australian cruiser HMAS *Sydney* and heavily damaged. The commander of the *Emden*, Karl von Müller, decided to run his ship aground in order to avoid sinking.

CHAPTER FOUR. THE ENGLISH STATE AND ENGLISH CULTURE   37

Englishmen withdrew from the Liège fortress,[10] they extended their hands to our field-greys: as the football player does after a completed match! And were surprised when they were given the fitting reply: namely, a foot in a certain part of the body.

Nowhere does the complete commercialisation of the war appear so clearly as in this unconscious confusion of war and sports. For sports is born from the innermost soul of the trader, who can never understand war. I shall say why. We need only keep in view the cultural values and life customs of the trader to find the answer.

※

What then has been brought forth in cultural values, apart from the monstrosity of the state and a hypertrophy of the economic apparatus, in this 'England Warehouse' since Shakespeare?

Far be it from me to speak of that which is called 'religion' in England; it indeed corresponds basically to that which one has the audacity there to call 'philosophy'. In any case, in this field, if we do not wish to cite the Salvation Army, no creative action has been accomplished by the English. That already the ideas of the Reformation were imported foreign wares, 'made in Germany', they have not made us forget till today. But what they have in turn understood in a masterful manner was the adaptation of their *soi-disant* metaphysical needs to their trading interests. God has been incorporated in the general business enterprise in a quite excellently skilful manner. The English have indeed become 'tolerant' in religious questions: that is far more reconcilable with profit-making and the comfortable life than an obstinate orthodoxy. We wish to recall here that Cromwell already allowed the Jews into England because he thought he may need them for his finances and the English trade. We also do not wish to forget that, in the famous Declaration of Indulgence of James II of 1687, which is admired as the Magna Carta of religious tolerance, it says literally:

---

10   The Belgian city of Liège was besieged by the Germans from 5 August 1914 and surrendered on 16 August.

'persecution was unfavourable to population and to trade': religious persecutions are not favourable to the interests of industry and trade. So we must ascertain the primacy of commercial interests even in the ecclesiastical policy of this nation.

Poetry? Apart from a couple of Irishmen: the Lord Byron who was driven out of the country by calumny, who cursed his nation thoroughly, and the likewise banished Shelley who solemnly renounced his native country in *Laon and Cynthia*.[11]

Fine arts? The sentimentalities of Gainsborough and Reynolds and the hysterias of the Pre-Raphaelites.

Music? ...

No spiritual cultural value can grow out of trade. Not now and not ever. But they do not even want any spiritual culture. All spiritual values oppress them. And that is why they have out of their innermost being borne two forms of life that may serve as substitutes for spiritual values, but which through their standardisation also help to eradicate the last relics of spiritual life from the people: I mean comfort and sports.

Since I shall speak in another context — thoroughly! — further below about these two plagues of mankind, let it suffice here to have mentioned them.

Fairness, however, demands that it should be stated that in these fields of material culture the English have really been promoters and enhancers. Just as they have — what does not need to be highlighted for the first time — at least in earlier times, essentially enriched our stock of technological and economic expertise. We shall still have to examine if these sole gifts of this nation have been a blessing for mankind.

---

11 *Laon and Cynthia; or, The Revolution of the Golden City* (1817) was the original version of Shelley's poem *The Revolt of Islam* (1818).

PART TWO

GERMAN HEROISM

CHAPTER FIVE

THE GERMAN MIND

WHEN FOREIGNERS philosophise about the present war they strangely always come back to the single idea: the war of 1914 is Nietzsche's war. Germany kindled it and Germany was inspired to do that by the spirit of Nietzsche. That is — when we disregard the untruth that we alone wanted the war — not incorrect. But it is one-sided. Just as one can call this war Nietzsche's war, one can call it also the war of Frederick the Great, or Goethe, or Schiller, or Beethoven, or Fichte, or Hegel, or Bismarck; it is indeed the German war. And Friedrich Nietzsche was only the last singer and seer who, come from heaven, announced to us the myth that the son of God would be born among us, whom he, in his idiom, called the Superman.

Nietzsche was only the last who spoke to our conscience, perhaps with some different words, but in the same sense as all our great Germans before him and as, indeed, only a German could ever speak, even when he wished to be considered rather as a 'good European'. But what else did he preach to us than that we should not lose ourselves in the base and common that creeps up to us from below, but whose breeding ground no other saw so clearly as Nietzsche as lying beyond the realm of German minds. Even if he defended himself often, and totally, from being compared with people before him, we, who look back with calm eyes on the harvests of past times, know that

Friedrich Nietzsche, with the best things that he said to us, is a native of Potsdam[1] and Weimar,[2] both of which taken together are the hometowns of the German mind. (They lie in the centre of Germany, whose peripheral ends are formed by Königsberg and Vienna.)

Is this German mind then something uniform that can be described in one word? The enumeration of just those four cities, along with which Wittenberg and Hamburg and Cologne and Munich also would like to maintain their claim, may make the attempt to determine the German character unequivocally seem hopeless. Ranke[3] once exclaimed:

> Who wishes to capture in concept or words what is German? Who wishes to give a name to it, the genius of our centuries, the past and the future? It would become only another phantom that would seduce us into other rocky paths.[4]

The Germans 'elude definition and are for that reason the despair of the French', said Nietzsche, who considered it a characteristic of the Germans that, among them, the question 'What is German?' is never exhausted. And perhaps the only thing that one finds in all German life is the eternally changing, the eternal being something else, for which reason the German is not something that is but eternally becomes, the endless diversity, the inexhaustible wealth in individuality and particularity, of the 'abyss of individuality', as it was called in the exuberance of Romantic speech.

---

1   Potsdam, adjoining Berlin, is the seat of the Prussian royal family of the Hohenzollerns.
2   Weimar, in central Germany, was the centre of German Classicism, the late 18th century literary and philosophical movement, which included such luminaries as Goethe, Schiller and Herder.
3   Leopold von Ranke (1795–1886) was one of the most important German historians of the 19th century and his œuvre includes several impressive scholarly histories of Prussia, France, England and Italy.
4   Leopold von Ranke, *Historisch-politische Zeitschrift*, Hamburg, 1832, I, 'Über die Trennung und die Einheit von Deutschland'.

To be sure, that would be already much that one could say about the German soul. But it seems to me that one can characterise more precisely individual characteristics of the German mind that sharply differentiate it from all others and that especially allow one to distinguish a very definite German worldview, just as we can without difficulty discern a specifically English worldview.

German thought and German feeling express themselves first in the unanimous rejection of everything that approaches, even from afar, English or Western European thought and feeling. With innate dislike, indignation, outrage, 'deep disgust', the German mind has raised itself against the 'ideas of the 18th century', which were of English origin; every German thinker who thought in a German way rejected utilitarianism, eudaimonism, thus, all philosophy of usefulness, happiness and pleasure; in this the adversarial brothers Schopenhauer and Hegel,[5] and Fichte and Nietzsche, Classicists and Romanticists, the thinkers of Potsdam and of Weimar, thus, old and new Germans were one.

To cite the sayings of just two German thinkers, who in many ways seem sharp opponents in their ways of viewing life (and yet are basically so related!), let us examine how Fichte and Nietzsche judge the vulgarity of English thought:

> Through the new education ... the training towards the pure will should be the first thing ...
>
> He (the pupil) should not at all hear that one can be impelled and move for the sake of one's maintenance and welfare, and as little that one studies for that reason, or that studies could in any way help that.[6]

---

5   Cf. Nietzsche, *Beyond Good and Evil*, 252: 'In the battle against the English-mechanistic stultification of the world Hegel and Schopenhauer (along with Goethe) were of one mind, those two opposed brother geniuses of philosophy who strove between themselves for opposite poles of the German mind and thereby did an injustice to each other, as only brothers do.'

6   *Addresses to the German Nation*, Second Address.

> Badness consists in loving only one's material welfare and in being moved only by fear or hope for that, whether in the present life or in a future. (Fichte)
>
> So I shall speak to you of that which is contemptible: but that is the last man ... 'We have found happiness', say the last men and blink.[7]
>
> Whatever is of a womanly type, whatever derives from the slave type and especially the vulgar mish-mash; this now wishes to be the master of all human destiny — oh, disgust! disgust! disgust!
>
> This is asked over and over again untiringly: 'How does one maintain oneself best, the longest and most comfortably?'
>
> Overcome for me, you higher men, the prickly ant-hill, the pathetic comfort, the 'happiness of the greatest number' ...![8] (Nietzsche)

And what do we set against that shopkeeper's ideal? Is there an affirmation that is found consistently in every German-orientated worldview? I think yes. And if I were to express what it is in one sentence I would like to cite the old seaman's saying that is inscribed over the shipping house in Bremen and says:

> Navigare necesse, vivere non est

'Life we don't need, but if we live, we have to do our damned duty and obligation'; or 'Man has to perform his work so long as he lives'; or 'individual life: our destiny is to create significance for the whole'; or 'the welfare of man is not important so long as he serves a cause', or however one wishes to translate this saying; it comes down always to the same thing. And no matter which German one asks, for his opinion he will answer with the saying that is inscribed over the shipping house in Bremen; the ordinary man who now fights for Germany in the trenches as well as the minds that serve as beacons to us:

---

7   *Thus spake Zarathustra*, I, Prologue.
8   *Ibid.*, IV, 'The Higher Man'.

CHAPTER FIVE. THE GERMAN MIND

> It is not necessary that I live; but indeed that I do my duty and fight for the fatherland to rescue it when it is to be rescued.[9] (Frederick the Great)
>
> Try to do your duty and you will know immediately what you are worth.[10] (Goethe)
>
> Let us add now the observation of the human race ... Even here life does not present itself in any way as a gift to be enjoyed but as a duty, a task to be performed.[11] (Schopenhauer)

Nietzsche (who is always especially valuable to me as a crown-witness for German thought and values because he is considered by superficial readers perhaps as an opponent of the German character and differently formed than the earlier great Germans):

> What is happiness worth? I have for a long time not striven for happiness. I strive for my work[12]
>
> What is the greatest that you can experience? That is the hour of contempt ... the hour when you say 'What is my happiness worth? It is poverty and filth and a pathetic comfort.[13]
>
> We (immoralists) have been woven into a tight net and shirt of duties and cannot get out of it — for that reason even we are 'men of duties'! It is true that sometimes we dance in our 'chains' and between our 'swords'; more often it is no less true that we grind our teeth and are impatient at all the secret harshness of our fate. But, do what we may, fools and appearances speak against us: 'those are men without duties' — We always have fools and appearances against us![14]

---

9   Frederick II, letter to Jean-Baptiste de Boyer Marquis d'Argens.
10 *Wilhelm Meisters Wanderjahre* (Wilhelm Meister's Travel Years), II, 'Betrachtungen im Sinne der Wanderer' (Observations as a traveller).
11 *Die Welt als Wille und Vorstellung* (The World as Will and Representation), II, Ch. 28.
12 *Thus Spake Zarathustra*, IV, 'The Honey Sacrifice'.
13 *Ibid.*, I, Zarathustra's Prologue.
14 *Beyond Good and Evil*, Sec. 226.

It has perhaps been said: such a worldview is the origin of our speculative philosophy, and then Kant brought us the 'categorical imperative' of duty. That is certainly false. Already the citation of German names whose bearers lived before Kant and who nevertheless represented the same morality demonstrates that this derivation is false. It would mean doing injustice to Kant too and misunderstanding totally the spirit of his doctrine if one were to maintain that he established definite moral principles and taught definite laws regarding a view of life. No, just as he claimed only to have discovered and not invented the forms of knowledge, so too he did not establish the moral law autocratically but merely exhibited it in its forms and, to be sure, also pointed to its suprasensual source. One knows the fine passage, the only one in which the Kantian style also acquires something like *élan*, where he derives the divine origin of the consciousness of duty from rational bases:

> Duty! Thou great and noble name, etc.... what origin is worthy of thee, and where does one find the root of thy noble source ... It can be nothing less than that which elevates man above himself (as a part of the sense-world), which connects him with an order of things that only the understanding can conceive, and at the same time has under it the entire sense-world, with its empirically determinable life of man in time and the totality of all ends (which alone is suited to such unconditioned practical laws as the moral). It is nothing else but personality, that is, freedom and independence from the mechanism of all of Nature; yet, regarded at the same time as a faculty of a being that is subject to special laws, namely, purely practical laws given by its own reason, the person, thus, as belonging to the sense-world, is subject to his own personality insofar as it belongs at the same time to the intelligible world; here then it is not to be wondered at if man, as belonging to both worlds, must necessarily observe his own being, in relation to its second and highest destiny, with reverence, and its laws with the highest respect.[15]

---

15   Immanuel Kant, *Critique of Practical Reason*, I, Ch. III.

That is really the great accomplishment of German philosophy that it — and only German philosophy, whereas that of all other countries was stuck in the categories of the understanding — had set itself the task of spinning threads through the power of reason from our life on this earth to that serious, quiet realm of spirits from which we come and to which we go, that it searched for the suprasensual in reason itself and in this way created genuine philosophy for the first time.

This German philosophy raises itself really and through the accomplishment of its thought to the unchanging 'more than infinity', as Fichte expressed it in a great way, and finds in this alone its true being.

> Time and eternity and infinity it sees in its origination from the appearance and manifestation of that One, which is itself simply invisible and is rightly apprehended only in this invisibility. Already infinity is, according to this philosophy, nothing in itself and possesses no real being; it is merely the means whereby the only thing that exists, and exists only in its invisibility, becomes visible and through which an image, a sketch and shadow of itself is formed within the imaginational realm. Everything that, within this infinity of the imaginational world, may become more visible is now fully a nothing of a nothing, a shadow of a shadow, and merely the means whereby that first nothing of infinity and time itself becomes visible and thought is allowed to fly to the being devoid of images and visibility.[16]

In brief poetic lines this idea is expressed then thus:

> Everything transient
>
> Is only a likeness[17]

As if Goethe could have thought even one bit more 'realistically' or, better, 'materialistically' or 'naturalistically' than the great representatives of German transcendental philosophy!

No: only he who hears the deep fundamental note of German poetry ringing out from this belief in the two worlds to which we men

---

16   Fichte, *Addresses to the German Nation*, Seventh Address.
17   Goethe, *Faust* II, V.

belong seems to me to fully exhaust its significance and value. We live two lives on earth: a lower sensual and a higher spiritual. In the first we are differentiated, in the latter united. And the entire meaning of the course of earthly life is that we rise from that lower sensual life into the higher one of spirit in which we become one again with the spirit world from which we originate. Therefore the overcoming of life, the duty of life, is that which we should accomplish. In strange accordance two of our greatest poets tried to express this purgation and raise of sensual man to the higher forms of life of spiritual man in words that everybody knows:

> And as long as you do not have this,
>
> This: die and become,
>
> You are only a shadowy guest
>
> In the dark world.[18]

And Zarathustra speaks:

> You must burn yourself in your own flames: how did you wish to become new if you have not first turned to ash?[19]

That is indeed the fundamental idea of Nietzsche's philosophy, which often gestures in words in a monistic manner and whose thought, however, was deep down transcendental. Otherwise, his doctrine of self-overcoming, which he announces as the final wisdom, would not have any meaning at all: we would want then to reduce his ideal of the Superman into a simple-minded ideal of breeding. Let us listen to the wonderful words of Zarathustra:

> Much is more highly valued by the living than life itself ...

---

18   Goethe, *West-östlicher Divan*, 'Buch des Sängers', 'Selige Sehnsucht'.
19   *Thus Spake Zarathustra*, I, 'The Way of the Creative Person'.

> Even the greatest thing gives itself and devotes life for the sake of power. That is the dedication of the greatest thing, that it is a gamble and a danger and a throw of the dice for death ...
>
> And this secret life itself spoke to me: See, I am that which must itself be overcome ...[20]
>
> Go, with my tears, into the isolation, my brother. I like him who wishes to go beyond himself and in this way perishes.[21]

What else is expressed in these words than that which the Faust idea teaches us likewise. In dedication is perfected the destiny of man, in the 'giving up' of himself by which he goes beyond the limits of his corporeality and unites himself once again with the realm of spirits: he returns to his home.

In this way the idea of duty too finds its most profound foundation. In the German language, and only in it — the only 'original language', as Fichte put it — one word it seems to me contains the entire significance of our thought and writing and striving: the word 'duty'. We have a duty to fulfil so long as we live, a duty that is broken up into a thousand daily tasks. Life is a duty insofar as it is given to us by a higher power. But by pouring out the content of our life we give ourselves up to our works, and this giving up of our own self gives us the only deep contentment that earthly life can offer; gives us our spiritual peace, because through it we perfect that union with the divine, being separated and torn from which constitutes our deepest sorrow and suffering on earth.

But it is the clearest characteristic of our German thought that we perfect the union with the godhead already on earth and perfect it, not through the mortification of our flesh and our will, but through powerful action and creation. That the giving up of ourselves occurs through constant positing and perfecting of tasks in active life gives our worldview triumphal power, gives it invincibility on this earth.

---

20 *Ibid.*, II, 'Self-surpassing'.
21 *Ibid.*, I, 'The Way of the Creative Person'.

That is why I call it also a heroic one, and now the reader sees to what point I have led him: *to be German means to be a hero*, and against the English trader's mentality in thought and life we set a heroic German one.

Trader and hero: they form the two great opposites, form as it were the two poles of all human orientation on earth. The trader, as we have seen, enters life with the question: Life, what can you give me? He wants to take, wants to get for himself as much as possible in exchange for the least possible action, wishes to make of life a profit-making business; that causes him to be poor. The hero enters life with the question: What can I give life? He wishes to gift, wants to dissolve himself, wants to sacrifice himself — without any return; that causes him to be rich. The trader speaks only of 'rights', the hero only of duties that he has. And even when he has fulfilled his duty, he still feels inclined to give:

> A fulfilled duty is always felt as a debt, because one has never done quite enough.[22] (Goethe)
>
> Thus do the type of noble souls want it: they want nothing gratuitously, least of all life.
>
> One who is of the rabble wants life gratuitously; but we to whom life has given itself — we think always of what we can give in return.[23]
>
> That is your thirst to sacrifice yourself and to become gifts; that is why you have the thirst to heap all wealth within your soul.
>
> But it is a horror to us the degenerating sense that says: everything for me.[24]
> (*Thus Spake Zarathustra*)

But the virtues of the hero are the opposite of the trader's; they are all positive, life-giving and awakening, they are 'giving virtues': self-sacrifice, loyalty, guilelessness, respect, bravery, piety, obedience,

---

22 *Wilhelm Meister's Travel Years*, 'Observations as a Traveller'.
23 *Thus Spake Zarathustra*, III, 'Old and New Tables'.
24 *Ibid.*, I, 'The Bestowing Virtue'.

goodness. They are warlike virtues, virtues that experience their full development in and through war, just as all heroism grows to its full stature only in war and through war. To comprehend that we must attempt to acquire some more insight into the character of the heroic worldview. We shall have to become acquainted with the intellectual direction that all heroism on earth necessarily takes and that passes over into the idea of the fatherland and the idea of the state.

CHAPTER SIX

THE GERMAN IDEA OF THE FATHERLAND

THE HEROIC CONCEPTION of life culminates directly and necessarily in a feeling for the fatherland. No heroism without a fatherland, but as one must equally say: no fatherland without heroism. For which reason the English trader nation does not even have a word for 'fatherland', the idea of which is alien to it.

The heroic worldview, which can also be called the idealistic, culminates, as we saw, in the disdain for the naturalistic individual life, whose calling it sees in giving oneself up, sacrificing oneself, to win a higher life in the spirit instead:

> Don't put your hope in life,
>
> You will never win life …[1]

Thus everybody serves the matter, his work, a supraindividual thing, and produces therewith a world over and outside himself. But in order that the effect of the individual not be without significance it must combine into a living unity in a higher life; out of the individual creation of the individual a total work must grow, which has its own life

---

1   Friedrich Schiller, *Wallensteins Lager* (Wallenstein's Camp), Sc.XI.

and which lives its own life on this earth, which is the genuine reality in this world, whereas the individual life is only like a shadow that flits past. This supraindividual life, for which and in which the individual lives, is represented in the idea of the nation or the fatherland.

The conviction that we are called to this whole that lives above us, that exists even without us and against our will to live and die, that only its life is real life because it is a life in God and in spirit; this moral consciousness forms the content of the idea of the fatherland and has nothing to do with the sentimental dependence on the 'homeland' and the 'soil'. But it also has nothing to do with the national pride of the English that is without any spiritual and moral foundation. This English national feeling that produces pride in every individual in belonging to such a 'powerful' empire as the English can best be compared to the pride of a clerk in being employed in the biggest and most respectable warehouse of the city. That the English national feeling has nothing in common with the German love of the fatherland is seen from the fact that it stops where the latter begins: namely, with the sacrifice for the fatherland. The drumbeat goes now throughout England to call the young English to the flag so that they may defend the fatherland. But not a single person follows the call out of an obvious sense of self-sacrifice. One who allows himself to be recruited does it because he considers it an advantageous affair.

A goodly providence rules over the fate of the German nation, which is destined for the highest on earth. It has raised it on the crooked ways of an unhappy political history to the heights of a heroic worldview and our nation owes to the errors of its political life even the spiritually and morally deepest idea of the fatherland and love of the fatherland.

It has been a blessing for us that, in the centuries in which the Western European nations developed into powerful state structures, in the time when the external world was divided, we stood apart and that, because we were forced back from all external power, we were free to conquer the realms of inner man. When the English Empire stood completed, within whose borders all true humanity was withered, at the end of the 18th century, within the realm of the German character, the free intellectual-moral man achieved his perfection:

the ripest son of the age.[2]

What he lacked in external power, the German had won in inner force.

And this same misery of political Germany developed now also the deeper and richer conception of the nation and the love of the fatherland. To be sure, it seemed for a while as if the German mind wished to fly over the limits of everything national and the love of the fatherland and follow the phantom of an anti-national cosmopolitanism. But this danger was avoided by the sure instinct of the German feeling. Already in those years of pure Weimar culture the conviction had impressed itself in the heads and hearts of our best that man is rooted in the national, draws his force from it, and is obliged to return his best to it. That logically necessary culmination of the heroic-idealistic worldview in the love of the fatherland had already been perfected at the turn of the 19th century in men like Wilhelm von Humboldt[3] and Schiller. In the example of Humboldt one sees, as Friedrich Meinecke especially felicitously pointed out in a fine chapter of his book on *Cosmopolitanism and the National State*, how an individualism that is honest and strict with itself must reach entirely through its own force and self-reflection to the recognition of the supraindividual powers of life, 'by which the individual life is surrounded and restricted but also borne and fructified'.[4] 'Man', it says in a Humboldt work of 1793, 'is, taken alone, weak and can accomplish only little through his own short-lived power. He requires a height on which he can place himself,

---

2   Schiller, 'Die Künstler' (The Artists).
3   Wilhelm von Humboldt (1767–1835) was a liberal Prussian philosopher, linguist, educational reformer and founder of the Humboldt University in Berlin.
4   Friedrich Meinecke, *Weltbürgertum und Nationalstaat* (Cosmopolitanism and the National State), Ch.III: 'Wilhelm v. Humboldt in den neunziger Jahren des 18. Jahrhunderts'.

a measure that is right for him, an order in which he can incorporate himself. But he achieves this advantage unfailingly the more he propagates the spirit of his nation, his generation, his age in himself.' And, on 18 March 1799, he wrote to Goethe: 'As you know the limitedness of my nature, you must feel that to me everything that may surround me outside Germany must indeed remain heterogeneous ... One who occupies himself with philosophy and art belongs to his fatherland more naturally than any other ... Philosophy and art that have formed a feeling and mental disposition for themselves and through which they have been formed again are more in need of their own language.'

And Schiller lets Attinghausen in *Tell*[5] speak the words of warning regarding the fatherland which strongly teach the duty of patriotism even today.

But, to be sure, the patriotism of the Weimar thinkers had a special complexion: it fully lacked a political character. It was what I earlier characterised as cultural patriotism. Love of the German people, German culture, love of the fatherland of the Germans, not really German love of the fatherland. For, how extensive could this have been in that age when political Germany experienced its deepest degradation? So the patriotism of that age bears a markedly apolitical stamp that speaks most clearly from those fragments that were found in Schiller's posthumous works in which we glimpse a plan for a poem, 'German Greatness' and in which it says:

> Separated from the political, the German has founded for himself his own worth and, even if the imperium collapsed, the German worth still remained uncontested. It is a moral greatness, it lives in the culture and character of the nation which is independent of its political fates ... when the political empire shook, the spiritual formed itself ever more strongly and perfectly.[6]

---

5   See Schiller, *Wilhelm Tell*, Act II, Sc. 1. The aged Baron von Attinghausen is one of the staunch patriots in the play, which is set in the 14th century during the Swiss struggle for independence from the Habsburgs.

6   Schiller, fragment, 'Deutsche Größe' (German Greatness).

One hears in these words the undertone of pain that every German must feel when he considers the misery of the political empire. But there is an overtone of pride in the unique spirituality of the German character. And that all patriotism of that age could express itself only as cultural patriotism, that is what I said deepened the German idea of the fatherland and the German love of the fatherland, that is what lent German patriotism for all time that special stamp, which we are today rightly so proud of. German patriotism sinks its deep roots in the fruitful soil of a heroic worldview, and around its crown shimmer the rays of the highest intellectual and artistic culture. As Friedrich Meinecke expressed it in a felicitous formula: 'By purifying the idea of the nation of everything political and, conversely, putting in all the intellectual wealth that one had won, it was raised into the sphere of the eternal and of religion.'

CHAPTER SEVEN

THE GERMAN IDEA OF THE STATE

IT PROVES THE WEALTH of the German spirit and the power of the German love of the fatherland that this people, as a whole stateless until recently, produced from itself an idea of the state of a profundity and worth such as did not exist since the days of Plato. An idea of the state that, to be sure, had to be produced with compelling necessity from the German heroic worldview as a logical development and which again set itself, outstanding in its monumentality, against the English shopkeeper's conception of the state.

A German conception of the state, I say. Not in the sense that it had ruled the intellectual world of the Germans at all times. We lived entire epochs in which the English trader mentality had spread itself wide in Germany and the doctrines of St. Manchester were announced to us. Here I do not think of the state theories of German thinkers who in the 18th century likewise took the doctrine of a state contract as the point of departure of their entire state doctrine. It would mean then desecrating the memory of Pufendorf,[1] Thomasius,[2] Wolff,[3] Kant if we wished — because they paid homage to the ruling fashion of the contract theory — to equate them to the shopkeeper minds that were keen, in their theories, to dissolve the state into a general trading business. In spite of the formal agreement of their state theories with the English, their mind was still German and a world separated them from the English theorists. Let us recall, for example, that the *jus naturae* of Christian Wolff starts from the duty of the individual, on which alone the rights of the individual are built: '*jus oritur ex obligatione; obligatio est prior jure, et, si nulla esset obligatio, nec ullum jus foret.*'[4]

But one would certainly do Kant in particular a bitter injustice if one were to throw his state doctrine — because it contains the contract element — into one basket with the mercantile theories, whose fundamental idea is, as we saw: to determine the utilitarian reasons why the individuals might have an interest in the state. The 'equally sophistic and worthless talk of the purpose of the state', as Rodbertus[5] expresses it, is completely lacking indeed in Kant's state doctrine. When we read, for example, what he says about the differentiation into active and passive citizens, when he states that the passive citizens (that is, those persons who are compelled to maintain their existence not through their own business but at the behest of others) are 'merely

---

1 Samuel von Pufendorf (1632–1694) was a German philosopher, who developed the doctrines of Hugo Grotius on natural and international law in his *De jure naturae et gentium* (1672).
2 Christian Thomasius (1655–1728) was a legal and political philosopher of the German Enlightenment.
3 Christian Wolff (1679–1754) was the most important German philosopher between Leibniz and Kant. His works range from mathematical and philosophical to legal, natural scientific and theological dissertations.
4 Christian Wolff, *Jus naturae methodo scientifica pertractatum* I, Cap. 2, 24,25: '*Quoniam jus oritur ex obligatione ... obligatio prior est jure ... Nullum igitur jus foret, si nulla esset obligatio*' (Since law arises from obligation ... obligation is prior to law ... Therefore, there would be no law if there were no obligation).
5 Johann Karl Rodbertus (1805–1875) was a German socialist, who belonged to the Centre Left Union in the Prussian National Assembly.

stooges of the commonwealth' 'because they must be commanded or protected by other individuals and hence do not possess any civic independence', or when he says, 'The source of the highest authority is for the people … practically inscrutable, that is, the subject should not … reason about this source when he is employed', and that the statement, 'All authority is from God' does not express a historical reason of the bourgeois conception but an idea, in the form of a practical rational principle, and the like, he still demonstrates sufficiently that he has intellectually nothing in common with the mechanistic-materialistic-individualistic state theories of Western Europe.

But smaller minds have peddled the English conception of the state among us, to be sure, not without being beaten down every time with heavy blows.

I am thinking of the time at the end of the 18th century when Mr. von Schlözer in his *General Constitutional Law*[6] could write: 'The state is an invention, men made it for their well-being just as they invented fire offices'. At that time arose among the 'Romantics' the first opponents of this inferior conception of the state, who also for the first time set up another German conception against it with full vigour.

So Adam Müller can be examined in the following:

> The state is not a mere manufacturing business, dairy, insurance institution or mercantile company; it is the inner binding of the entire physical and intellectual needs, of the entire physical and intellectual wealth, of the entire internal and external life, of the nation in a large, energetic, endlessly moved and living whole.[7]

---

6   August Ludwig von Schlözer, *Allgemeines Staatsrecht und Staatsverfassungslehre*, 1793. Schlözer (1735–1809) was a historian, who specialised in Russian history and constitutional law.

7   Adam Müller, *Die Elemente der Staatskunst*, Zweite Vorlesung, Berlin: J. Baxa, 1809.

And to let another Romantic express himself, I wish to present here how Novalis[8] already expressed himself with almost complete profundity and purity, with poetic illumination, rejecting everything that the apostles of happiness had philosophised into the state as a mutual insurance institution:

> All culture arises from the relations of a man with the state ... Man has attempted to make the state a cushion of indolence, and yet the state should be precisely the opposite — it is the armature of the total activity; its goal is to make man absolutely powerful and not absolutely weak, not the laziest but the most active being. The state does not remove effort from man but it multiplies his toil infinitely, of course not without multiplying his power infinitely.[9]

Then there came a dreary period for Germany when, in the 1860s and 1870s, the representatives of the so-called Manchester School peddled their imported wares quite shamelessly on the German streets as German products. I have already pointed out how they were reprimanded by the socialist Lassalle, with whom the socialist Rodbertus was associated. And it is well-known how this 'Manchester theory' has been contemptuously discarded today by theoreticians and practitioners in Germany as fully failed and useless. So that we may perhaps say that, in the conception of the state, the German mind has even reached sole mastery in Germany. Or does the Manchester spirit still haunt many minds?

If we ask now in what the German idea of the state consists, we shall have to characterise the German conception of the state as an objective organic one to indicate that it starts from the fundamental idea: the state was neither founded nor formed by individuals, is not an aggregate of individuals, nor does it have the goal of promoting any interests of the individuals. Rather more is the state the community

---

8   Friedrich von Hardenberg ('Novalis') (1772–1801) was an influential German Romantic poet and philosopher, who opposed the doctrines of the Enlightenment with a spiritual vision of humanity.

9   Novalis, *Schriften*, ed. Ludwig Tieck and Friedrich Schlegel, Berlin, 1802, II, 'Fragmente vermischten Inhalts', III: 'Moralische Ansichten'.

of the people, it is the conscious organisation of something supraindividual, to which the individuals belong as parts. If the heroic worldview had advanced to the recognition of the supraindividual existence and power of the community of people, it had to reach this idea of the state, as I have already said, because the living mass of the nation could become conscious of itself and make its nature objective to itself only in the form of political unity.

Because it is often attempted by the opponents of this German conception of the state to devalue it by branding it as 'reactionary' and setting it against the 'progressive' theory of the state of the English trader's mentality, I wish to present here once again the words of Ferdinand Lasalle in which he makes known his view of the nature of the state (following the theory of his teacher Fichte) ("Workers' Programme", 36):[10]

> The state is this unity of individuals in a moral whole, a unity that multiplies a million times the power of all individuals who are included in this unification ... The goal of the state is therefore to bring the human character to positive and progressive development, in other words, to form human destiny — that is, the culture that the human race is capable of — into a real existence; it is the education and development of the human race to freedom. This is the actual moral nature of the state, its true and higher mission.

'Development to freedom': that means, in the Fichtean sense, the freedom of the individual to form himself to the moral perfection that he already possesses as an ideal person, that is, to become really, approximating to the idea, that which he is in the ideal realm. 'However great the differences that separate me and you from one another, gentlemen', Lassalle apostrophised his judges at the end of his famous defence speech before the appeal court, 'in relation to this resolution of morality we stand hand in hand! The ancient vestal fire

---

10 Ferdinand Lassalle, *Über den besonderen Zusammenhang der gegenwärtigen Geschichtsperiode mit der Idee des Arbeiterstandes*' ('Das Arbeiterprogramm', April 1862) Berlin, 1863.

of all civilisation, the state, I defend with you against the modern barbarians (the Manchester men)!'[11]

Most closely bound to this idea of the state is the concept that the individuals have, with regard to the whole, first, and especially, duties, and rights for the individual may be derived only to the degree to which they correspond to fulfilled duties. This conception of the state rejects likewise in its logical implementation the schematic, purely quantitative, equal evaluation of the individuals and posits as the ideal the ability of the individuals different in their capacities and achievements to come together in a manner beneficial for the success of the whole for the development of their nature. This conception means therefore (at least I would like to express it thus) an organic one, not, as one mostly supposes, because it compares the state to an organism in the biological sense (this analogy should rather be omitted or applied with the greatest caution; it leads astray easily; also because, in every case where one is captivated by a political theory, one attributes it to the objective-organic in the sense of the conception of the German constitution, which is in no way permissible: thus the state theory of Hobbes is born completely out of the English, not German, mind) but it means therefore rightly an organic one that is opposed to the mechanical English one because in it the relation of the individuals to the whole is conceived in an 'organic' sense insofar as the individuals in the spiritual sense should join themselves to the spiritual whole in an 'organic' manner. If you like, it is a question here too of a comparison with the organism in the biological sense but indeed with a completely different understanding. The state is indeed also a living being but a metabiological one, a spiritual living being in which the individuals participate through their spiritual life.

Without, moreover, ceasing to remain individuals or to preserve their value as independent individuals. That is the difference between the ancient and the German conception of the state. Against

---

11   Ferdinand Lassalle, *Die indirekte Steuer und die Lage der arbeitenden Klassen*, Zürich, 1863, p. 136.

the Manchester idea of the state, Lassalle again said to the workers, in Germany 'there fights strongly the classical education that has become the inalienable foundation of the German mind'. But it is the characteristic of the German conception of the state that it does not allow the individual to be swallowed up by the state but attempts to reconcile German individualism and Christian self-esteem with the idea of the ancient (and, incidentally, also French!) omnipotence of the state.

We wish to bear in mind a fine statement of Fichte that warns of the excessive overstretch of the idea of the state; he says once in his addresses:

> The German clarity has ... perceived with an unshakeable conviction that ... no injury and no mutilation of the individual can be healed by the glory of the entire nation.[12]

But he certainly does not mean that the individual must remain 'safe' while the reputation of the nation above it is ruined. The higher living being remains always the state and the state should take care precisely that it exists as a living being. The state is the mighty armour that the nation puts on to defend itself against hostile forces. Nation and people would also externally disintegrate soon if they were not protected by a strong state: that is, as it were, the problem of the state observed from outside. But this leads us directly to the problem of war that stands in the closest intellectual relationship to everything dealt with up to now.

We must become clearly aware of the fact that a national state necessarily presupposes the existence of other states and can exist only through it. This fruitful idea was perhaps first expressed by Adam Müller, who gave it the following formulation:

---

12 Fichte, *Addresses to the German Nation*, First Address.

How may all the numberless individuals of whom the state consists come to the recognition that they form a whole if other states, other political entities, did not remind them of their correlation and force them to the community that they form.[13]

The nature of every state demands incessantly to assert itself as a living entity, to constantly compare and measure itself to other states. But especially its organic expansion is also necessary for the activity of a living being: in every state there lives 'an inner pressure towards vital growth, fully unconscious to the present generation but deriving from the impetus of earlier generations,'[14] as Adam Müller once again expressed it in a perfect manner.

A 'living growth' takes place in an organic state; a dead, purely commercially grounded expansive tendency does not rule it, as we were able to observe in the mechanically pieced together English world empire. That all the forces, all the organs, all the limbs of the state, should constantly remain in a harmonious relation to one another, this conviction forms likewise a firm component of what we have encountered here as the objective, organic, or German idea of the state.

This idea of the organic individual life of every state enters instead of the shopkeeper's idea of a dead balance of the individual states amongst themselves; an idea that contains within itself all the necessary guidelines for a healthy state policy, which I do not, however, wish to pursue further here. There will be more to say about that later.

It should just be mentioned that the battle of nations amongst themselves, that is, international war, forms an unavoidable accompanying phenomenon of all political life, so long as it is a life. The justification of war lies in the natural condition of all living things, to which the states must belong, '*quella guerra è giusta, che è necessaria*,'[15] said the man who was to teach a world of shopkeepers. The opposition between traders and heroes is resolved here into the opposition between shopkeepers and warriors, between whom we must choose.

---

13   Adam Müller, *Die Elemente der Staatskunst* (Berlin, 1809), Zehnte Vorlesung.
14   *Ibid.*, Erste Vorlesung.
15   Niccolò Machiavelli, *The Prince*, Ch. 8.

CHAPTER EIGHT

GERMAN MILITARISM

He values battle, our enemies have declared, as we have seen. And we said they were right. But what is this militarism? On this Germans and foreigners will be of very different opinion. The announcements that the latter have issued in the last months against militarism do not really attest to a deep understanding of its nature. If I disregard what Prof. Larsen in Denmark or Dr. Gino Bertolini in Italy have said about German militarism (one or two more may be added to them, whose statements escape me), one can characterise everything that foreigners placed in high positions and low have said about that recently as nonsense, without being unfair. Another proof of the fact that a foreigner cannot understand us, apart from a very few prominent personalities whom a happy fate has raised to the heights of the German mind.

How fully the thought of non-German men, especially those with a trader's mentality, fails in the case of a problem like that of militarism — for that, once again, Herbert Spencer is an eloquent example.

Spencer posits, as we have already seen, the two social types, the militant and the industrial, against each other, naturally esteeming the former as the lower and the latter as the higher. But how he describes the militant social type shows that he too has not the least idea of its character (whereas he analyses the 'industrial type' with a fine trader's instinct). What he says about it are nothing but superficialities; thus he is able to characterise the 'fundamental principle' of the militant type as nothing but 'compulsory cooperation' (*Principles of Sociology*, Art. 554).

The fundamental fault of his conception, as well as of that of all foreigners (which is always in these matters one 'dedicated to death', as Fichte put it), is that they consider a certain institution as the primary cause from which a certain spirit is supposed to emanate, that they thus invert cause and effect, since there is indeed only a certain spirit whose external phenomenal form is the social or political institution. All well-meaning foreigners always want to liberate us from some 'institution'; the president of Harvard University, Eliot,[1] would like to draw up a better constitution for us so that we may slowly work our way up with diligence and perseverance to the cultural level of the USA. Others would like to free us from our Kaiser, who is supposed to weigh upon us like a burden. The aim of most, however, is to 'liberate' us from militarism. The same false basic view returns repeatedly: as if all these institutions that are found among the Germans, like a burden that weighs upon a donkey, were something external. Whereas it is important to understand that all external manifestations of social and political life are the necessary radiations of the spirit that informs a people.

Thus militarism too is at first, naturally, something external because it is institutional. It is represented in the universal compulsory military service; is represented in the powerful military force, against which now the whole of Europe and half of the rest of the world battle in vain; is represented in numerous barracks and their more or less pleasing 'blooms': military parades, machine guns, walrus moustaches, standing at attention, and many uniforms.

But all that is only the outer costume. What manifests itself here is produced by a certain spirit that has more far-reaching effects than the

---

1 Charles William Eliot (1834–1926) was President of Harvard University from 1869 to 1909.

eye perceives, that infuses our entire people and operates in thousands and thousands of vital expressions, in all fields of our public and private life, our outer and inner life. What therefore, we must ask, is this spirit that produces militarism or which itself appears as militarism?

What else can German militarism be than the German spirit that we have recognised? It is this German spirit, one can perhaps express it thus, in its living activity, in its formation into external life-forms. Militarism is the manifestation of German heroism. Militarism is the realisation of heroic principles, especially insofar as it deals with the preparation and implementation of wars.

Militarism is the heroic spirit heightened to the warrior spirit. It is Potsdam and Weimar in deepest union. It is 'Faust' and 'Zarathustra' and Beethoven scores in the trenches. For even the 'Eroica' and 'Egmont Overture' are indeed the purest militarism.

But if we ask in detail what it is, in order to obtain a full insight into its character through a tangible comprehension, one will be able to point to the following components in the military spirit.

First of all, one must understand by militarism that which may be called the primacy of military interests in the country. Everything that is related to military matters has priority among us. We are a nation of warriors. The warriors merit the highest respect in the state. Which appears externally in so many things that strike foreigners: our Kaiser obviously always appears officially in uniform, on festive occasions even our highest bureaucrats and officials do the same if they are placed in a military position; the princes are born, so to speak, as soldiers and belong to the army from youth. All other branches of national life serve military interests. Especially the economic life too is subordinated to it, etc.

The second characteristic of militarism is the veneration and care of all warlike virtues, especially of the two basic virtues of the warrior: bravery and obedience, the true virtues of the free man. It is strange with what accordance our great moralists repeatedly preach these two virtues. I think of Hegel, I think especially of Nietzsche:

What is good? you ask. Being brave is good ... Rebellion — that is the excellence of slaves ... Your excellence is obedience! Your command itself is obedience.[2]

Self-control and discipline are the fruits of the care of these virtues: order inside and order outside, that is a fundamental feature of German militarism. Here too Potsdam and Weimar have joined together to teach us that. An essential component of the Goethean character is surely the strong sense of order that he inherited from his father. Note the similarity of the fathers of our greatest Weimar thinker and our greatest Potsdam thinker! The external organisation of our army then resulted in the fact that spiritual and physical discipline have infused all the strata of the nation and in this way forms even in a real sense a strong component of the national spirit. Not only in the domain of the army; in all fields of our public life and in the private life of every German this spirit of breeding and order has made its home. Whether it is a matter of the primary schools or the universities, the trades unions or the central bank, the railways or science, it is always the same spirit, it is always German 'militarism' that informs them, before which the foreigner stands as before a wonder. For from this spirit are the gigantic works of organisation produced that have surprised the world in this war.

But it would be to characterise German militarism only imperfectly if one did not wish to bear in mind yet another feature in it that has similarly manifested itself now especially clearly once again: I mean the living pressure to a commitment to the whole that informs every German when the fatherland is in danger. What is included, as we have seen, in every true heroic worldview triggers militarism as it were; it awakens the heroic feeling in the breast of the least daily-wage worker in the village, it popularises the ideas that arose first in the heads of our greatest thinkers. The idea of the fatherland becomes a life-awakening force only through the intermediary role of militarism.

---

2   *Thus Spake Zarathustra*, I, 'War and Warriors'.

What heroism means in the deepest sense is placed living before the eyes of the intellectually poorest when he goes to war in rank and file with his comrades in order to defend the fatherland.

The spirit of militarism is transformed here into the spirit of war. Only in war does the spirit of militarism, which is indeed a warlike heroism, develop itself fully. And only in war does its genuine greatness become manifest:

> As soon as the state calls out: now it is a question of me and my existence, there awakens in a free people the highest of all virtues that cannot prevail in such a great and unrestricted way in peacetime: self-sacrifice. The millions are together in the one thought of the fatherland, in that common feeling of love unto death that, once experienced, is never forgotten and ennobles and consecrates the life of an entire generation. The conflict of parties and classes yields to a sacred silence; even the thinker and artist feels that his ideal creation would only be a tree without roots if the state were to collapse. Among the thousands who go to war and selflessly obey the will of the whole, everyone knows how miserably little his life is worth next to the glory of the nation.[3]

But because all virtues that militarism highly esteems achieve fullest development only in war, since true heroism, whose realisation on earth militarism ensures, operates only in war, war appears to us, who are filled with militarism, as a sacred thing, as the most sacred thing on earth. And this high esteem of war itself then forms an essential component of the militarist spirit. Nothing is considered more suspicious in us by all traders than the fact that we consider war as sacred.

They say: war is inhuman, it is senseless. The slaughtering of the best of a nation is bestial. So it must seem to the trader who knows nothing higher on earth than the individual, natural human life. But we know that there is a higher life: the life of the people, the life of the state. And we know for that reason with deepest sorrow in our hearts that the individual life is destined to sacrifice itself for the higher life

---

3   Heinrich von Treitschke, 'Das constitutionelle Königthum in Deutschland', in *Historische und politische Aufsätze*, III, Leipzig, 1903.

if the latter is threatened. With this belief, and of course only with it, the painful dying of thousands acquires a meaning and significance. In the death of a hero the heroic conception of life finds its highest consecration.

> The promise of a life, even down here, beyond the duration of life down here — this alone is that which can inspire one to the point of death for the fatherland.[4] (Fichte)

> One who goes to death for his fatherland is free of the deception that limits life to one's own person; it extends one's own life to one's fellow countrymen among whom one continues to live, even to their coming generations, for whom one works; whereby one considers death as a blinking of the eye that does not interrupt one's vision.[5] (Schopenhauer)

> What are possessions and property in life?
>
> All things that pass!
>
> That we quiver with enthusiasm,
>
> When we rise to war,
>
> That will last forever,
>
> That is willed by God!
>
> God is courage in troubles,
>
> Is the nobility that drives us;
>
> Honour, loyalty, discipline, conscience!
>
> People, you feel enraptured because
>
> Your spirit remains immortal:
>
> The spirit of God! (Richard Dehmel, written in the war year 1914)

This highest feeling that the human heart can experience, that one goes to death for the sake of life, has been celebrated by poets in thousands

---

4   Fichte, *Addresses to the German Nation* (Berlin, 1808), Eighth Address.
5   Arthur Schopenhauer, *Preisschrift über die Grundlage der Moral* (1839), Part IV, Ch. 2.

CHAPTER EIGHT. GERMAN MILITARISM

and thousands of songs. We are a nation that is rich in war songs and in these war songs our warrior spirit, our militarism, is manifested once again, as it were, with brilliant clarity. What an abundance of living war songs has sprung up in these days in the German nation, which are all tuned in the ancient deep manner:

> There is no finer death in the world
>
> Than of one who, struck down by the enemy
>
> On a green heath in a wide field,
>
> Can no longer hear loud laments.[6]

But thousands of times heroism itself makes itself manifest once again. We can look with admiration upon victorious army leaders. We begin to believe once again in the greatness of man and we are overcome with shudders of lofty emotion when we receive news of the deeds and sufferings of our young heroes out there before the enemy and even feel the fate of these young brilliant men consecrated to death among our own relatives. To what heights of loftiness the heroism rises in deed and disposition is shown by the following little story which may be recorded here as a representative of thousand similar ones, as evidence to later generations of the greatness of our age:

The Hungarian staff sergeant Widery of the 66th Infantry Regiment held, with 51 men, an important railway tunnel against all the assaults of the Russian army in Galicia until the withdrawal of the Austro-Hungarian troops had been effected without hindrance. Then, through a betrayal, a Russian detachment of a thousand men fell upon the brave group from behind. The small troop did not think of surrendering and continued to fight. All but three fell. The 85-year old father of Widery, a former police officer, announced the death of his 24-year

---

[6] Song from the time of the Thirty Years' War of the 17th century, set to music by Friedrich Silcher (1789–1860). It was published in 1909 in the collection *Der Zupfgeigenhansl,* which was popular in the Wandervogel and Jugend movements.

old son in the following manner: 'I do not publish this information with a black ribbon because it can only awaken praise and joy that Sergeant Stephan Widery, my only son and comrade in the world war, was able to die for the fatherland.'

How many generations come and go in peacetime to whom it is not given to experience such an elevation of the soul as is granted, like a gift from heaven, to every reader of these few lines.

But war is sacred to us not only because in it the noblest characteristics of human character are impelled to flower; we do not consider it less sacred because it appears to us as the greatest moral force that is employed by providence to preserve men on earth from dissipation and indolence. Nobody has described this moral influence of war with more apt words than Heinrich von Treitschke:

'Every nation', he says,

> most of all a finely-formed one will fall victim easily in a long period of peace to weakening and selfishness. The unlimited comfort of society is the downfall not only of the state but at the same time of all the ideal wealth of life. The bourgeois mentality or cosmopolitan activity, which has in view only the satisfaction of all the pleasures of the individual, undermines the foundations of a higher moral worldview and the belief in ideals. Superficial minds come to the nonsense that the life-purpose of the individual is acquisition and enjoyment, that the purpose of the state is nothing but the lightening of the business of its citizens, that man is destined to sell at a high price and buy cheap, that war, that disturbs him in this activity, is the greatest evil and the modern army only a sad relic of mediaeval barbarism. For such a generation it is a sufficient blessing if fate were to send it a great and just war, and the more sweetly the comfortable custom of merely social life cajoles the heart of man, so much more powerful seems then the repercussion that raises it to warlike activity in the service of the state.[7]

We can summarise these words in our sense by saying: war, which forms the perfection of the heroic worldview which grows from it, is necessary so that this heroic worldview itself be not plundered by

---

7 Heinrich von Treitschke, 'Das constitutionelle Königthum in Deutschland'.

the powers of evil, by the creeping trader's mentality. It, a child of this worldview, gives birth to it, in turn, from its own womb. But this view of war is not really just a result, as is sometimes maintained, the result of our new German development. Not just the Germany of Bismarck and Moltke spoke of war as sacred. As long as German men have taken a position on the problem of war, they have placed faith in the conception that emerges in the words of Schiller:

> War is terrible, like the plagues of heaven,
>
> Still it is good, a gift like them.[8]

The sad work of the aged Kant on 'eternal peace',[9] in which not the great philosopher but the one intimidated by the lamp of death, crumpled and exasperated shipowner Kant from Königsberg speaks, forms the only infamous exception. Otherwise, pacifistic expressions are not known to me from any age. They would mean always a sin against the holy spirit of Germanness, which from the depths of its heroic mentality cannot reach anything but a high evaluation of war. Not only for a certain cultural epoch in whose limitation even a Herbert Spencer accepts blessings on war but now, and in all ages, until the kingdom of God on earth will be realised.

What a folly to believe that this 'religion of barbarism', as our moral evaluation of war is called abroad, is only born of the Potsdam spirit and is the product of a war-addicted officer clique, is only a fall from the good traditions of our thinkers and poets. No: Potsdam and Weimar are on this point once again fully in accord. I already presented the words of Schiller, who repeatedly praised the beneficial effects of war, which he calls the 'mover of the human race'. We still remember the wonderful passage:

> ... Man withers in peace,

---

8   Schiller, *Wallensteins Tod*, Act II, Sc. 2.
9   Kant, *Zum ewigen Frieden*, Königsberg, 1795.

> Idle repose is the grave of courage,
>
> The law is the friend of the weak,
>
> It wishes only to make everything equal,
>
> Would gladly flatten the earth;
>
> But war lets force emerge,
>
> Raises everything to a lofty level,
>
> Gives courage even to the coward.[10]

But even Goethe did not think differently:

> Do you dream of the day of peace?
>
> Dream who may dream,
>
> War is the watchword,
>
> Victory! and thus forever.[11]

It would be a devaluation of a poet to attribute pacifistic sentiments to him. As if, within the sphere of influence of pacifistic ideas, anything like poetry in general could bloom. Or does one indeed think that Beethoven's music could have sounded out from the trader's peace-loving mind? One who considers such a wonder to be possible may read in his deathbed speech what the master thought of the 'Doric' key that is spoken of in Plato's *Republic*!

How far our 'classical' age, which one is wont to bring into opposition to the modern German character, was from all disregard and repudiation of war is proved by the attitude of so movingly quiet and reclusive mind as that of Jean Paul, who, however, called war: 'the strengthening iron therapy of mankind and indeed more of the part

---

10   *Die Braut von Messina*.
11   *Faust* II, Act III, Sc. 2 'The Inner Court of the Castle'.

that suffers than of that which triumphs'.[12] 'The traumatic fever of war, he means, is better than the prison fever of an indolent peace'.[13]

I could fill pages upon pages with citations of sayings of our great thinkers about war that are all tuned in the same way; especially our philosophers, the Fichtes, Schopenhauers, Hegels, Hartmanns, Nietzsches, no matter how much their 'systems' may contradict one another in other aspects, in their judgement of the purifying and elevating effect of war they are one. But why adduce yet more proofs for the fact that impresses itself on everybody, that to feel and think German means to bless war. But, to be sure, only 'real war', as Fichte called it, which moves the entire nation and is borne by the entire nation and is conducted for the maintenance of the state. Only such a war, that is arisen out of noble impulses, can also bear in itself the moral force that brings a healing and strengthening to the nation.

That we also consider the aims of war to be sacred and do not abuse them, like the trader nations, to defend vain commodities, that occurs with similarly compelling necessity from our reverence for this highest disciplining and training instrument of God.

Nowhere more clearly does the opposition that prevails between militarism and commercialism, between the heroic and the trader's worldview, appear than in their fundamentally different attitudes to war.

---

12 Jean Paul, 'Friedens-Predigt an Deutschland', 1808. Jean Paul (Johann Paul Richter) (1763–1825) was a German novelist of the Romantic period.
13 Jean Paul, *Mars' und Phoebus' Thronwechsel im Jahre 1814*.

PART THREE

THE MISSION OF THE GERMAN NATION

CHAPTER NINE

LIFE BEFORE THE WAR

THERE IS NO DOUBT that the trader's culture was about to conquer the world for itself. Just as the trader's mind had created an economic system suited to it, capitalism, so it used the latter in turn to find entry with it into all countries. Yes — there were circles in which the strong conviction ruled that, to the degree to which the capitalistic economic system spread over the earth, even the trader's spirit and with it the trader's culture would become the ruling ones all over, to which view, therefore, all of mankind should be led. I myself have not been far from these circles, as the final chapter of my *Bourgeois*[1] reveals.

So much is certain: mankind was infected with the trader's worldview first in England. But the English sickness had then spread further around it and had especially infected also the German national body.

If we bring to mind the condition of our cultural life before the outbreak of the war, we remember clearly that in it essential components of the English culture had begun to spread. I say 'essential components of the English culture', which could produce the erroneous impression that, out of a rich abundance of English cultural products, we had appropriated some by choice. In reality, we were able

---

1   Werner Sombart, *Der Bourgeois*, München: Duncker und Humblot, 1913.

to determine already that the modern English 'culture' disposed of generally only two products (apart from economics and technology, which these days bear an international stamp) that present themselves as original English products, and it is a question of taking over only these two: comfort and sports had come over to us.

But we must now become aware of the fact that these two — sole! — products of the English trader's culture are inimical and detrimental in the highest degree to true culture, that they are apt to destroy radically any higher, loftier ethos, that they are, however, especially so dangerous to all heroic, thus true, culture because they are introduced as harmless life forms, as an enrichment of the finer, nobler life, and employ their destructive influence on the national organism only after some time, after they have installed themselves in it.

Comfort means first of all nothing but making life comfortable. And that such a thing is basically harmless, and that we all accept it without hesitation and gladly, cannot be doubted. When the oven does not smoke and the windows close tight that is certainly a good condition. One can also agree that a prettily decorated tea-table and a clean bath are conveniences of life that are in themselves not apt to erode any lofty view of life.

But it is equally certain that they bear within themselves great dangers. Already, when one begins to attribute some importance to them instead of considering them as infinitely incidental things to which one should pay as little time and attention as possible. It saddened me when I read in a report of a German soldier from the battlefield in a Berlin newspaper, how the writer wrote with definite respect of the shaving kits that were found among the English soldiers even in the trenches. That is sad: in the midst of such great events to have reverence for the removal of beard stubble from a handsome face. Every shaving kit in the trenches seems to me to be, rather, an ugly emblem of the empty English shopkeeper's culture.

But now, when indeed comfort begins to seize a broad space in the conduct of life and evaluation of life, when the orientation of life, under the standpoint of greatest comfort and convenience, becomes, so to speak, one, if not the only, component of a worldview, then it is a harmful poison. Then comfort destroys all idealistic impulses, and it destroys also all artistic culture. Our comfortists often confuse artistic and decorative culture, of which the latter can at most be combined with comfort. But an overgrowth of decorative arts is itself detrimental to all fine artistic culture. Just as it obviously contradicts the idea of true art that the idea of utility and comfort be combined with it in any way. What one admires therefore in the English salons in England — and elsewhere — has nothing in the least to do with art, no matter how pleasing the tasteful arrangement of everyday objects and pieces of jewellery in a room may be. But we wish to separate fully the concepts of comfort (decorative arts) and art! That the English could become the reformers of modern decorative arts has its principal reason perhaps in the complete desiccation of their artistic life. All artistic epochs of history, the ancient Greek, the period of the Middle Ages, the Renaissance, the Baroque, the Rococo, were periods without comfort.

Now, comfortism as a worldview is certainly evil, and a nation that is filled with it, like the English, is not much more than a heap of living corpses. The entire national body becomes putrid. For one should not think that comfort is a lifestyle that extends to the small elite of rich people. In England today, every trade union member is already stuck in the swamp of comfort. For comfort is indeed not an external form of life but a definite way of evaluating life forms. It is not found in objects but in the mind and so it can be spread over rich and poor alike. But it is so fundamentally dangerous because, in its retinue, other values creep into the soul that are apt to drag the latter into baseness. One who highly esteems comfortable and pleasant life must also allot a high value to material goods, and one who does that must view a great value in a wealth of material goods likewise. Whereby thus an inversion of all values would be reached that, if it were to become a general phenomenon in the nation, will cause devastating results.

How far we ourselves had gone in this deviation from all true culture in Germany before the war is still clear in everybody's memory.

Sports is the twin-brother of comfort. It comes into the world along with the latter. It too is in its basis and beginnings harmless and appears, in the form of physical exercises, even as a friend of every active young man. But in its further course, sports too shows itself to be a sickness that consumes the healthy organism, when, that is, it proceeds to take the place of other more important activities of life: when it, on the one hand, wishes to substitute soldierly exercise, and on the other, intellectual occupation — as it already does in England and as it had begun to do in Germany before the war.

Physical exercises in this form that overrides all other life values must necessarily cause the human soul to wither, make it dull, as it makes it physically a cripple, that is, a man with a partially developed muscular and vascular system. We have seen with horror the ravages that sports caused in many of our young people before the war and looked forward with trepidation to the time when our colleges would sink in the same way as in England to sports training institutions.

Sports rises, like comfort, to a worldview, sportism, according to which all of life is a sport or is divisible into individual sports. War as sports! We have already become acquainted with this disgusting spawn of the English shopkeeper's mentality. But the shopkeeper's mentality is actually the producer of sportism, in which all the trader's ideals are realised. Sports is, first of all, unwarlike and, for that reason, suited to the soul of the trader. But sports can also be so filled with the commercial spirit so that it develops as it were into a continuation of trading activities outside the counting house, which the calculating, profit-directed clerk can occupy himself with even on Sunday. This raising of sports into the sphere of commercialism is effected through the introduction of the bet, through which all sportive performances have received their financial expression. But then all interest in sports is bent into the purely quantifying interest of the trader; no longer is it a question of the how, the form of the performance, but of its external measurable success: this external success is registered in figures in the form of records.

Therewith records become the principal worth of the sportist and, to the degree to which sportism eats into the national body, the principal worth of life itself.

Once again we wish to recall with a shudder to what an extent such an intellectual orientation was spread even among us before the war. Who does not remember the hypnosis in which the Berlin population was set through the six-day race, who does not recall that fine summer day when literally half of Berlin was brought to its feet to watch the return of a race-car driver whom a Berlin newspaper had sent round the world for publicity purposes. For us that was just the beginning. And perhaps the sickness of sportism spread only in Berlin on a large scale. Still: there were worrying symptoms that could be clearly perceived of a general infection of the German national body too by this English poison.

More serious, posh natures who did not see principal merits in neither wealth nor in records wanted to know why they lived and so senselessly drudged on as the modern cultural business forced them to withdraw behind the 'idea of the profession', which, however, had also lost all deeper significance after its religious tip had been broken off. Finally one felt it as a sin against the Holy Spirit when one considered economic activity as a goal in itself. It was a devaluation of the idea of duty, but also of the idea of obligation, when one reached the point where one had to view as the highest and final goal the devotion to a stock company and its profit aims. But even one who performed higher work than spinning cotton and making colours remained isolated in his activity, as a specialist, as it were hovering in the air. The scientific and technological methods and skills became increasingly more specialised and sophisticated, but the combination into a meaningful whole was lacking. The differentiation was not followed by any integration. And so all professional activity also remained purposeless and meaningless.

All of life seemed purposeless and meaningless. And the terrible vision of the ant-hill rose before the mind's eye of the far-sighted. One saw mankind degenerate in good living, getting married, filling their stomachs and emptying their intestines, and running hither and thither without any meaning. One thought that one was near the condition that Mephisto described so seductively to old Faust as the highest:

> I loved to see the carriages,
>
> The eternal sliding back and forth,
>
> The eternal running here and there,
>
> The disturbed hill of swarming ants.[2]

Everything that we did seemed to have become purposeless and meaningless.

We heaped up riches upon riches and knew nevertheless that no blessing would flow from them.

We created wonders of technology and did not know why.

We engaged in politics, wrangled with one another, threw filth on one another: why?

We wrote and read newspapers; mountains of paper towered before us daily and pressured us with worthless news and even more worthless opinions; nobody knew why.

We wrote books and plays and critics in troops did nothing in their entire life but criticise, and cliques formed themselves and fought one another and nobody knew why.

We raved about 'progress' so that the meaningless life would be heightened still further; more wealth, more records, more advertisements, more newspapers, more books, more plays, more training, more technology, more comfort.

And the more cautious had to ask repeatedly: why?

---

2 *Faust*, II, Act IV, Sc. 1, 'High Mountains'.

Life had really become a playground slide, as one of its best commentators expressed it. A life without ideals means therefore an eternal dying, rotting, a stench, since all of mankind from which idealism has disappeared changes to putrefaction, like a body from which the soul has fled.

CHAPTER TEN

DESPERATE RESCUE ATTEMPTS

IN THE MIDST of so much filth there was also much goodwill and numerous were the attempts to rescue men from the morass into which the trader's mentality had lured them and to lead them up once again to the bright heights of the heroic view of life. For it was always a question of this either-or: the trader in the swamp that one may call commercialism, Mammonism, materialism, sportism, comfortism, or whatever, or the hero on the heights of idealism. In this way are God and the devil, Ahura Mazda and Ahriman, called for modern man.

But, however numerous the rescue attempts were, and produced through however much goodwill, they all failed and had necessarily to fail.

I think first of all of the many efforts to make individual men moral, to preach individual heroism. Certainly this or that soul may have been rescued by them. But in our age all preaching to reflection and atonement has passed over the great mass of people without a trace. One can at best preach 'monism' to them because it suits their instincts. But to move them to a reversal on the path of materialism through strong admonition? I do not believe in any success of such an approach. The lower instincts are too powerful for that, especially in our age, in which they are strengthened and are ever reproduced by the ruling economic system. What did the ethical admonitions to an 'ethical culture' produce? What did the doctrines of the Superman, propounded with powerful prophetic pathos, effect? Among lofty natures, who had of their own accord kept themselves from contact with the trader's mentality, they certainly brought about many benefits by making the path to the heights clearer and easier. But those were already strong men. And by the rabble of coffee-house *literateurs* precisely Nietzsche, whom they did not understand and therefore transformed into baseness, was misused to strengthen them in their epicurean life and in their trader's mentality.

And can religious preachers save men these days from sinking into materialism? I do not doubt that where the religious sense still has supremacy from past times a dam against the mammonistic flood has remained standing. But England, the original country of this mentality, indeed provides the best evidence that precisely a strictly religious, or better, a church-directed life does not protect one from being filled with the trader's mentality. One can therefore go every Sunday to church and still be — a trader. Nietzsche maintained simply that 'the Englishman, as the more common of the two, is also more pious than the German'.[1] In any case, the old churches must, if they wish to participate in the rescue work of modern man, become more conscious once again of the heroic aspect of their doctrine so that they may really form a bulwark against the powerful commercialism, and will have to make use of the strong ideal forces that have arisen once again in the love of the fatherland and in the idea of the state. On the other hand, I do not attribute any force to the new 'religions' that spring up from the earth like mushrooms to achieve much in the battle against the evil of our age. Here is still valid what Frederick the Great once said to such a founder of a religion when he said: 'All very admirable, my dear; what is only lacking is that you nail yourself to the cross for it.'

---

1 Nietzsche, *Beyond Good and Evil*, 252.

CHAPTER TEN. DESPERATE RESCUE ATTEMPTS

Of much greater importance are all those efforts that wish to raise men through the presentation of a social ideal, thus everything that can be summarised under the collective name of 'socialism'. Doubtless, socialism is in our age one of the strongest idealisms to which one owes many rescues from the poverty of the trader's mentality, but which is, as experience has shown, incapable of implementing the rescue work; which has now already forfeited an essential part, if not all, of its power of redemption, and which in any case will never be by itself strong enough to rescue us from the evil.

The weakness of the socialist ideal is easy to recognise: it is related first to the fact that its ideal is an ideal of the future. To dream of the latter has naturally no significance for a formation of life. Only when it must be fought for can it fructify a life and awaken life. Now, the socialist ideal is indeed in this sense a practical one and in the battle for its realisation it has produced all the idealism that radiates from it. And we do not wish to consider as little the fullness and power of this socialistic idealism. The young people among the Russian revolutionaries, the German Social Democrats who experienced the *Sozialistengesetz*:[2] those were heroes, no matter what one may think of the political justification of their efforts. But the precondition of this social idealism is clearly its revolutionary foundation. It is the fanaticism that grows from the will to transform an existing condition, through force, into another. Without this high tension of the will towards action, the force of this idealism soon languishes. For which reason we can observe repeatedly in history that revolutionary parties 'moulder'.

But modern socialism is not less subject to this danger of 'mouldering' than all the other similar efforts that preceded it. And that is why it is faced with the bad alternative: either remain 'revolutionary' and therewith fully forfeit its practical penetrating power, or to

---

2   This anti-socialist law was passed in 1878 by Bismarck (in reaction to two unsuccessful assassination attempts on Kaiser Wilhelm I in that year) and enforced until 1890.

adapt itself to the existing conditions and therewith lose its idealistic momentum.

The attempts to unite the impossible, that is, to preserve, in a party that is capable of government with a revolutionary spirit, an idealistic momentum that is well nourished, must collapse with an inner necessity.

All heroic idealism that socialism has hitherto brought into the world has been an idealism of battle. It has consisted in the fact of individuals sacrificing themselves for a supraindividual thing.

To the degree that the goal was moved to a distant time and a direct (revolutionary) battle did not have a meaning any more, there was set in its place the means that were supposed to help on the way to peaceful reforms in order to reach the final goal: the party. There is no doubt that even today a good portion of the sense of sacrifice is awakened among the workers through the dedication to the party, by working for the party. Except that that too can only be a temporary condition. For a party is not a living whole like a nation into which all the vital currents of the individual flow together and from which the individual receives in return all life values. It is basically a dead organisation, which does not live its own life but receives life only through the dedication of its members, on the one hand, and, on the other hand, through the goal for the achievement of which it has been formed. If light does not emanate any more from this goal, the party organisation atrophies, the constant glorification of the mere means produces displeasure and in the routine of daily life even 'the most splendid feelings' ossify.

But now the greatest weakness of socialism lies in the fact that the final goal that one attempts to realise, that is, the actual socialistic ideal, is nothing less than lofty.

The basis of the inventory of ideals that socialism in its different groupings has at its disposal are formed, as is well-known, by the 'ideas of 1789': liberty, equality, fraternity, that is, genuine and actual traders' ideals that aim at nothing more than to obtain certain advantages for the individual. These were also the fundamental demands of the bourgeoisie and especially of the commercialised English bourgeoisie. And they are thus fully unsuited to form a heroic idealism upon. What was later added to this basis by way of specifically socialistic ideals also smells strongly of the trader's spirit: thus, for example, the demand that every worker obtain his 'fair' wages and things like that. Always only demands are set out, at least in those socialistic programmes that have predominated. And demands of individuals, we know, are always an emanation of the trader's mentality.

Whatever else has emerged of socialistic ideals is mostly confused. So, for example, when they have had the audacity to present Nietzsche's ideals as ideals of socialism. Under the catchphrase that socialism would allow every person to develop his 'individuality' into a total harmony. One who expresses such nonsense has first of all totally misunderstood Nietzsche. But he also has a most deficient notion of the 'formation of individuality'. As is well-known, this ideal was planted by many Weimar thinkers in the 'classical' epoch. But they, like Wilhelm von Humboldt and Schiller, did not understand it in the superficial trader's sense, that now everybody can do and permit everything that he wishes, but gave it a strict lofty significance so that its realisation amounted to 'that unique combination of the Platonic sense of beauty and the Kantian moral strictness',[3] as it has been expressed. This doctrine can, according to its nature, be comprehended only by lofty minds. As soon as it is flattened and generalised to a mass ideal, it ends in the worst eudaimonism and herd-instinct ideal. 'Individualism' is a dangerous word. It can mean the highest heroism and equally the lowest trader's mentality.

Not much better is the case of the 'humanitarian ideal', which likewise belongs to the components of the intellectual world of modern socialism. It is either only an ideal out of opposition to the patriotic and for that reason already fully sterile; or else it is only formal, rather

---

3   Heinrich von Treitschke, *Historische und politische Aufsätze*, III, 'Die Freiheit'.

in the sense of the Kantian formula that man can never be a means but always only an end, and then purports next to nothing, or else, when one wishes to give it a content, it eludes all imaginability since a mankind without the individualities of nation is a phantom. 'Mankind' however is, first of all, nothing that one can serve, that one can sacrifice oneself for, and with regard to which one can have duties. It is therefore completely unsuited as the object of a life-awakening ideal. The 'humanitarian ideal' can in the best of cases have only a negative sense.

But what especially has broken the redemptive force of socialism is that it, through a tragedy that should not be underestimated, has produced from it itself those forces that destroy all idealism in the socialistic movement and that have therewith cut off the life-threads of the latter.

The founders of modern socialism recognised rightly that changes of the social order that is built on interests can be introduced most quickly if one calls out to interests to battle for a new order. They thus took as the leading slogan for the socialist ideals the class interests of the proletariat. Now the socialist movement has become increasingly a movement for proletarian interests, and the actual socialistic ideals that were at first raised as moral demands have been pushed increasingly into the background.

But therewith the socialist movement has been filled completely with the trader's spirit. The goal now is: fighting for as many advantages as possible for the wage-earning classes. The battle has degenerated into an out and out battle for a share in the trough. 'What you have too much of, we wish to have' is the slogan. The 'prickly ant-hill', the wretched comfort, the 'happiness of the greatest number' has therewith become the goal of the socialistic movement. The socialism flattened in this manner, which now already coincides with the English trade unionism, which, like the latter, sees the real values of life in comfort and sports, is nothing more than capitalism or commercialism with inverse insignia.

CHAPTER ELEVEN

THE REDEMPTION FROM THE EVIL

ONE WHO HAS read the two preceding chapters will, even if he is not familiar with my earlier works, understand why I, and many along with me, and not the worst thinkers before the war, had fallen victim to a total cultural pessimism. We had acquired the firm conviction that mankind was at an end, that the remainder of its existence on earth would be a totally unpleasant condition of proletarianisation and reduction to an ant-hill, that the trader's mentality was in the process of infiltration everywhere and that the 'last men'[1] approached who say: 'We have discovered happiness and blink'.

Then the miracle occurred. War came. And a new spirit broke out from thousands of sources; no — no new spirit! It was the old German heroic spirit that had only smouldered under the ash and that had suddenly been kindled into a flame again.

Flame, consuming flame!

First it sprang up in the hearts and kindled here an enthusiasm never known before, never imagined in its magnitude. You have all experienced it. This devotion, this sense of sacrifice, this heroism that had arisen overnight in 70 million German hearts. You all have

---

1 See above p. 44.

experienced it, how the consuming flame of this love of the fatherland had burnt out everything petty, divisive, mundane in our souls, and how we all, pure and, as it were, newborn, set ourselves in the service of the whole.

But then this flame also illumined our heads. It rose like a sun over our lives, that lay in darkness, and immersed everything in its blessed light. Now we saw with living eyes: there was still something supraindividual, a whole, a life outside us: the nation, the fatherland, the state. And we felt once again *this* life as the *higher* one, as that from which alone our life was derived. We understood it as obvious that our life, just as it receives its consecration from that higher life, so it should be led for that higher life too, that all our actions and efforts had to be related to the flourishing of that higher one in whose lustre we lived. A source of inexhaustible idealistic heroism had arisen once again. And an ideal had come to life in the fatherland that was located in the mind, within the grasp of every man, even the poorest.

But that is the decisively important thing: here, in the love of the fatherland and, more precisely expressed, in the idea of the state is the only point at which an idealistic worldview can become a really general one of a nation. The idea of the political community to which one is joined as a serving member is, especially in wartime, conceivable by every man and the fulfilment of duty in the service of the externally visible political whole comprehensible to every man; that is why only this idealistic conception of the state, which is kindled by the flame of the love of the fatherland, can be the intermediary between the empirical individual being and the realm of the spirit. Herein lies its immeasurable and indispensable educative power.

If now the flame of the love of the fatherland has begun to burn in the hearts, and political idealism begun to illumine the heads, then life has obtained a significance again. What was disintegrating and collapsing is now, as it were, sustained. All goal-setting that previously broke down at a point and fell back with the question, 'why?', on our will, which was increasingly paralysed, culminates now in one highest goal: in the safety and growth and flowering of our nation and its state. But this goal is for us an absolute goal because here the godhead is revealed to us, and only in the union with it already on earth can the significance of life for every heroic worldview lie.

Everything now obtains a significance once again, our striving for a firm goal and a steady direction.

How we struggled with the population problem before the war! The question whether many or few men were better was pondered back and forth and answered with arguments of different sorts, sometimes in this sense at other times in others. Now there is no longer a population problem in the sense that it could be questioned whether many or few men, whether an increase, stagnation or decrease of the population, were to be wished for in our country. We know, rather, that we must have a strong increase in the population to be able to sustain ourselves as a national state, or as a state, in the struggle with nations. How do we, who have often turned up our noses at the swarms of people in our states, on the rabbit-hutch-like condition of many of our provinces, bless now these people when they roll in immeasurably thick columns to the frontier to defend our fatherland against presumptuous enemies! And also we know now how the men look who were born and grew up there. Vigorous, in every body's view.

But therewith the guidelines of all education are drawn up. Its task can only be: to train German heroes. Heroic men and heroic women.

This requires especially: that the body experience a full and harmonious training. I have earlier expressed my indignation at sports and sportism and characterised them as the bad English spirit from which we must protect ourselves. One will not consider me to be so foolish that I wanted to turn against the ever progressing custom of taking care of the body in sports and exercise. I have protested only against the unhealthy and one-sided development of this care of the body, against the excessive growth of sportive interests, against the atrophy and stultification through sports, against the promotion of sports through the trader's mentality, against the nonsense of records and similar products of the English nuisance, and the propagation of this English nuisance.

But, to be sure, we too — and more than any other nation — will take care to toughen the body and develop all the powers of the body in a harmonious manner so that we may see a generation of bold, broad-breasted, bright-eyed men grow up. For, the fatherland needs them. And broad-hipped women to bear capable warriors, strong-boned, brawny, persistent, courageous men so that they are suited to be warriors. I think that herein the principles according to which German sportive life, if we wish to use the foreign expression, should develop are outlined.

No very strong favouring of the specifically English sports: tennis, football, cricket, which are truly traders' sports because the warrior aspect is taken off from them. The caricatures of matadors in these sports should frighten us. We should leave them unenvyingly to the English. Whereby again I naturally do not wish to say that even all these sports as sports and practised on a reasonable scale are not harmless and welcome entertainments. But the German mark will be brought into physical exercises, for we prefer all those that have a final warlike aspect. Just as no Greek youth would have degenerated to English sports ideas but would have undertaken only those exercises in the gymnasiums that formed the entire body in a harmonious manner, so we too should see our principal task in genuinely warlike exercises or in activities that develop the entire body.

Hiking, racing, skiing, shooting, hunting, mountain climbing, rowing, swimming, fencing, discus throwing, gymnastics, riding, there are so many innumerable — and among them some genuinely German — possibilities to train our bodies that we really do not need to always practise only the English traders' sports.

But we wish to distinguish ourselves from the English also by the fact that we do not fully forget through the care of the body that of the mind. We wish to be aware that heroism in the final analysis is not active in the muscles but in our mental disposition. And we will take care to cultivate the heroic disposition in our youth so that they may learn to live and die for the fatherland. Education will have to make its principal task the cultivation of the heroic virtues, especially bravery and obedience and self-sacrifice. Naturally, we need in large numbers practical youth suited for useful actions in life, for the needs of life and so that German life may develop in a rich way in economics and technology. But even to those who cannot participate in the advantages of a humanistic education we wish to add a bit of heroism by teaching them that all the significance of life consists in fulfilling one's duty and in the individual's weaving at the tapestry of God, which is revealed to him in the form of his nation.

But, to the extent that the needs of life permit, our education should train men who are free of the world, who are more at home in the world of ideals than in the alleys of the 'big city'. Above all, we must still feel as the sole heirs of the Greek nation as well as of all antiquity and must always bear in mind that to educate young Germans indeed means filling them with a heroic German spirit, but that the heroic German spirit reaches with its roots into the people from whom Marathon and Salamis, Homer and Plato were born.

Politics? Will it rise once again from the degradations of petty interest conflict and the hairsplitting show of principles? It must. And it can, if it really takes the statement seriously: *salus republicae suprema lex*![2] A brisk party life is quite certainly necessary and desirable; it is a sign that the entire body of the nation and state is itself alive. But all party politics may be led by nothing but the ambition to take care of the well-being of the state. Every party claim must be formed with a reference to the interest of the whole, the nation, the state. It should never, in the demands of the parties, be a matter of the claims of individual groups or classes of the population, of the rights of individuals, of the interests of the businessmen or the propertied,

---

2   'The welfare of the republic is the supreme law'. This was a maxim of Roman law.

the producers or the consumers, the entrepreneurs or the workers, but always of the *salus republicae*, of the 'interest' of the *Reich* (state), of the commonweal. In order that it may be so, certainly much more of the sense of the objective-organic idea of the state must be appreciated than hitherto, and an end must be put to the pernicious trader's views of 'Western European civilisation'.

The fundamental features of all German politics are certainly fixed for the future as well: a powerful state armoured in steel and, in its defence, a free, vigorous people are its ideal. Free in the German sense, in which freedom means to be able to do one's duty according to one's own laws and of course also to be happy in one's own way. Thus freedom especially from the unbearable slavery to the public opinion under whose yoke the English nation groans.

And that every single person take part in the administration of the commonwealth in accordance with his powers and capacities.

But all professional life also now acquires once again a significance and a goal. Every single person completes in quiet fulfilment of duty his individual work, which is first incorporated into the entire work of his field of specialisation, and then is destined to become a benefit, or an ornament, of the German nation. Everywhere the principal point of view is the welfare of the whole. And all individual activities are, as it were, integrated in the harmonious beauty of the whole.

All economic activity is performed so that the organism of the German economy may flourish; but the German national economy is there to serve the state. How much more influence this principle must gain in the formation of our economic life has been shown to us once again by the war.

And now even technology may calmly continue on its path of conquest; now we are no longer afraid. Now we know why. The 42 cm Mörser,[3] the field-grey uniforms, the bomber and reconnoitring aircraft, the submarines, have once again revealed to us a significance

---

3   This was a siege mortar used by the Imperial German Army during the First World War.

in technological progress. We have also learnt to highly value the fact that our railways function so well since the time they brought Hindenburg⁴ through Germany to the Eastern Front in twelve hours so that he could win the battle of Tannenberg.⁵ Everything, I say, that seemed senseless previously has once again received a sense and significance since the time that its worth was derived from a higher worth, a worth that is the highest for us.

It is to be wished for that our intellectual life, our science and our art may likewise participate in this blessing that the idea of the fatherland has disseminated. May all snobism, affectation of things foreign, all art for art's sake, all spiritualism, all literary pomposity, all cold skills be swept away by the storm wind that now roars through our country. And may, above all, the devil take three-quarters of our 'intellectuals', our 'creators' when there is the opportunity. So that we feel a little less 'spirit' all around us in the future and, for that reason, obtain more 'poise', to use the appropriate word of Schnitzler's.⁶ But that the tree of German culture may bear blossoms even in the future, that is, produce deep works of philosophy, art, science we hope always.

And that, along with the orientation to the idea of the whole, our effort to form strong, distinctive personalities closed within themselves — who are indeed the most superb ornament of a national culture — should remain undiminishedly strong is obvious.

We Germans always have 'Faust' in our heads — we may think and attempt what we wish. Thus, since I glance at the future of Germany, the words, the last words of the dying Faust, hover before my mind and I wonder if Goethe's legacy perhaps coincides with the ideas that now fill us:

---

4   Paul von Hindenburg (1847–1934) was the German general who commanded the Imperial German Army during the First World War. He later served as President of Germany from 1925 until 1934.
5   The Battle of Tannenberg was fought between Germany and Russia in August 1914 and ended in Hindenburg's victory over the Russians.
6   Arthur Schnitzler (1862–1931) was an Austrian Jewish author of plays and novels with highly erotic content.

Such a bustle would I like to see

With a free people on a free land.[7]

That sounds almost like the swarm of prickly ants, from which, however, Faust himself had already turned away with disgust. But the words lose this sense and acquire the direction that I have just pointed to as the direction that the development of the German mind should take when we add the adjacent words that are too often forgotten:

That is the last word in wisdom

Only he deserves freedom and life

Who must conquer it daily

And so, surrounded by danger, lives through

Childhood, manhood, old age here throughout his vigorous year.[8]

'Surrounded by danger': that is the last word in wisdom.

For, without danger, man becomes atrophied and superficial and invents happiness. (That is perhaps one of the reasons why the English nation has decayed to the degree that it represents itself to us today: that it did not know danger for so many decades and centuries.)

Now Goethe's Faust constructs a 'danger' for the little people, which, of course, every pacifist must welcome, that indeed is so much after his heart: in order to remove it, it is sufficient to dig dams instead of swinging swords. But unfortunately, the Goethean construction is outside all reality. For one thing, we cannot all live in flood plains; for another, life in flood plains itself has, thanks to technology, become free of danger. Just as indeed in the remaining lands all natural dangers are removed through the enormous apparatus of our social safeguards. Everybody is indeed 'insured' today against any danger.

---

7   *Faust*, II, Act V, Sc. 6, 'The great outer court of the palace'.
8   Ibid.

At most, here and there a profession still carries some danger with it, like the miner's profession or the pilot's. But for the whole, that is today no longer threatened by the plague and cholera, the little 'danger' does not suffice to preserve it from the real danger of turning into an ant-hill. There is only one danger that is a universal danger: that is the threat to the fatherland from external enemies. It therefore is part of the ideal image that we make of the future German nation which, in addition to its many blessings, has a share also in the fact that it lives in the midst of enemies and for that reason is, in the true sense, 'surrounded by danger'. That we must be even for reasons of 'security', which even the trader values, for all of the foreseeable future a nation of warriors — that is the surest guarantee that we will also remain a nation of heroes in the sense that we have given to the word.

But with that I come to the last problem that should still occupy us here: what will, what should, the position of Germany be among the nations, and to the nations, after the war?

CHAPTER TWELVE

WE AND THE OTHERS

THE ONLY RELATION that we maintain now with the principal nations of Europe is war and the only important thing is at this time nothing but that we win, win essentially and decisively.

Perhaps it has been said against me that these admonitions to a rejection of the trader's spirit fundamentally do not at all support the will to win, which is indeed a product of a strong national feeling. You should have rather wished that Germany as a political structure become once again as weak as around 1800, for at that time was that worldview formed that you commend to us. Your ideals indeed coincide with the desires and plans of well-meaning foreigners who give us Germans the good advice to return once again to our kingdom in the clouds and to leave the earth and the seas to the other nations.

You err, my friends, when you raise such objections to me. To be sure, I think, and have myself expressed it in these pages, that that state-less time a century ago was a blessing for the Germans, who were able in this period to deepen themselves when the other nations became more superficial. But what can arise without a state, a strong, deep national culture, cannot exist without a state because it would fall prey to the other states. What becomes of stateless peoples or those with weak states, for that the 'small' nationalities of Europe provide sufficient evidence. The state is like an armour that must protect the tender national body, like the hard, strong husk that surrounds the ripe fruit. That was understood even at that time when we were without a state by the men of the classical period, and nobody expressed it with more apt words than the mature Humboldt, who had as a young man written such a passionate work against all states. He expresses himself in a work in honour of Stein in 1813 (cited by Meinecke, p. 185):

> Germany must be free and strong not merely because it can thereby defend itself against this or that neighbour or generally against any enemy but because only a nation that is strong even externally preserves the spirit in itself from which all the blessings inside it too stream; it must be free and strong in order to nourish, even when it is faced with a test, that necessary self-assurance to be able to follow its national development calmly and undisturbed, and maintain in a lasting manner the beneficent position that it assumes in the midst of the European nations.

No, my friends, you confuse materialism with realism; to be sure, the former is not reconcilable with an idealistic worldview, but the latter is. We wish to be idealists but not ideologues, not sailors in the clouds but remain firmly on the earth and take as much from the land and the sea as we need for our existence and our normal growth, not more, but also not less. Our kingdom is of this world. And that precisely is the special characteristic of the conception represented here: that we place the strongest reality on this earth, the will to power that is embodied in the state, in the service of an idealistic worldview, that we cannot believe in its maintenance without such support as accrues to it from the idea of the state.

But, if we wish to remain a strong state, we must win. And even the objection that I hear is not justified: that for our spiritual deepening, for the salvation of our souls, an unsuccessful war would be more beneficial than a successful one. Of course, a lost war would lead to a return to inwardness, to remorse, but with more difficulty to an active life in the light of an idealistic worldview. And we strive for that still. For, only victory guarantees us the conviction that the good, the noble, moral greatness still has a dwelling-place on this earth, that this earth is not fully enslaved to the trader's mentality, that all power is not contained in money. Only a strong victory would give us an impetus and momentum.

But a strong victory produces for us also the possibility of not worrying further about those who surround us. When the German stands supported on his gigantic sword, clad in steel from top to toe, then there might dance around his feet whatever may, they may scold him and besmear him with filth, as they are already doing now, the 'intellectuals', the artists and scholars of England, France, Russia, Italy; he will not be disturbed in his sublime repose and will only think to himself in the manner of his forefathers:

> *Oderint, dum metuant.*[1]

But what will happen then, ask anxious intellects to whom German culture is still something foreign, to the vaunted 'internationalism' that we have been building so eagerly for decades and that signifies to us the only worth? I shall not be so rude as to reply bluntly: 'The devil take that!' ('and let him take you along with it at this opportunity!') but wish to reflect for a moment what really is to be understood by this 'internationalism' and what character it has.

Obviously, 'internationalism' encompasses very different things, that is, that the relations of nations to one another are indeed of a manifold nature. There we have, first, the material-economic relations, the economic 'division of labour' of nations among themselves. There is no doubt that this is a great problem in itself. But it does not belong to the intellectual scope of this work and therefore I do not have to deal with it in this place. I wish only to remark quite generally on this

---

1   'Let them hate me, so long as they fear me.' This statement is attributed by Suetonius (*Lives of the Caesars*, 'Caligula') to the emperor Caligula, though it may have been taken from the tragedian Accius (170–86 B.C.) (see Seneca, *Dialogues*, 'De ira', I,20).

subject that we must always have this sort of internationalism to the extent that we need it: for here the purely business interest, which is indeed the only one among our worst enemies, decides. Moreover, the war will make us more and more strongly aware that all international economic relations are a necessary evil that we should make as small as possible. Doubtless, the most urgent task of national economic policy after the war will be: to find ways and means through which we may attain as great an economic autonomy as possible.

Closely related to this economic internationalism is that which one can characterise as institutional or legal internationalism. It encompasses all the arrangements and contracts on any common or opposed interests, mostly derived from commercial life, of the different states. Here the endless series of conventions is to be mentioned, from the post and telegraph treaties to the international industrial protection laws and the Geneva Convention. This part of internationalism has doubtless instituted much good and may develop further in the future without disturbance. And it will, since it arose from the interests of the individual states.

Then there is a political internationalism, once again with different significances. It can mean the diplomatic relations of independent states among one another, thus 'alliances' of all sorts, which is naturally not the subject at hand; but it can also mean the efforts to blur the boundaries of the independent states and to introduce a political union of the members of the different ethnic groups. Even if there is perhaps no Anacharsis Cloots,² no 'orateur du genre humain',³ among the men running freely around, the idea of 'fraternising the nations', as we know, still haunts numerous minds and celebrates its festival in all international socialist congresses. That the international tendency of

---

2   Jean-Baptiste du Val-de-Grâce, baron de Cloots (1755–1794) was a Prussian aristocrat, who participated in the French Revolution promoting the concept of a universal brotherhood of nations. However, he was finally suspected of treason by the Committee for Public Safety and executed.

3   Cloots called himself the 'orator of mankind'.

the proletariat is, from the standpoint of the views represented here, only a harsh evil I do not need to express deliberately. To what extent our workers, who return home from the trenches, will be cured of this disease we must wait to see. And if they — what is desirable — will be strong enough to free themselves from that clique of international editors that has up to now imposed the hard yoke of internationalism upon them. It is to be hoped for that our German social democracy,[4] which, in spite of all the contrary statements, has nevertheless been the most patriotic — to the irritation of the radical internationalists at the different congresses: I think of the military debate in Stuttgart! — will now especially strike the national note of the workers' movement once again. Heartening signs that they wish to do this are already evident in many written and oral statements of the German social democrats.

There remains the cultural or intellectual internationalism, with which designation one can summarise all relations of nations to one another in scientific, artistic, social fields.

Thank God in the immediate future the range of international relations of this sort will be determined by enemy nations so that we ourselves do not need to worry about it. Still, it is good that we already know quite clearly what is at stake for us in a loss or restriction, or even a (later!) extension, of these relations.

Basically, from an intellectual-artistic viewpoint, we Germans need nobody. No nation on earth can give us anything worth mentioning in the field of science, technology, art or literature that it would be painful for us to do without. Let us think of the inexhaustible wealth of the German character, which includes everything in itself that human culture can produce in terms of real values. One does not need to be a German to perceive that.

---

4 The German Social Democratic Party was originally formed in 1875 as the Marxist *Sozialistische Arbeiterpartei Deutschlands* and, on the termination of the *Sozialistengesetz* in 1890 (see above p. 89), was revived as the *Sozialdemokratische Partei Deutschlands*.

But it is part of the German character (many call it a German bad habit) that we have always had a sense and love of foreign life. 'It would mean being un-German to want to be only German', it has been said. That is connected once again with our intellectual wealth. We understand all foreign nations, none understands us, and none can understand us. So we discover values in foreign cultures that we would like to make use of. And if in this supplementation of our life we maintain the right measure and definite guidelines, there is no doubt connected to it. Of course, we must — every one of my words calls that out as a warning — protect ourselves, as from a plague, from every manifestation of the trader's mentality, no matter in which field it may express itself. We must recognise as standing far below us everything that resembles 'Western European ideas', that is even remotely related to commercialism. Therefore we cannot at all 'learn' from any nation on earth in all questions of internal politics, the constitution and administration. We thank President Eliot[5] and all the others who are concerned to draw up a 'better' constitution for us from our hearts for their goodwill but declare with courteous firmness that we ourselves know best what is suitable for us from a political viewpoint and that we consider everything that at the moment is being discussed to death west of the German border in terms of constitutions as highly inferior.

That even the English constitution and administration, at whose altar our old liberalism has sacrificed, can no longer be, at least for us, a model, all experts have perhaps now perceived.

It is different in the scientific and artistic field. Here foreign cultures can offer us many stimuli. Can German science experience any advancement from abroad? Books that we read with benefit we obtain according to our heart's desire. The international scientific congresses will hopefully disappear in the foreseeable future; even if all international journals closed down, if the exchange of scholars were

---

5   See above p. 68.

to be stopped for a couple of decades, it would be no loss to us. There remains the 'stimulus' from foreign art and literature. If one understands by that that we wish to enjoy the products of foreign countries, there is nothing to be said against that. We can hardly be harmed by that. If one understands by that that foreign artists, foreign poets are cultivated and promoted by choice in Germany, that is a nuisance that should hopefully disappear. If one understands by that, finally, that our creative artists allow themselves to be influenced, there lies in such a relationship a serious danger for German art, which really does not need such encouragements from abroad. I would like to hold before the soul of anybody that speaks constantly of the fruitful influence of foreign cultures on our German cultural life the words of Goethe — who, however, was certainly not a 'German nationalist' and not a 'chauvinist':

> The German runs no greater risk than rising with and through his neighbours; there is perhaps no nation more suited to develop from itself; that is why it was the greatest advantage to it that the world outside took notice of it so late.
>
> Now that a world literature is being introduced, the German, considered carefully, has the most to lose; he will do well to heed this warning.[6]

That foreign cultures offer us intellectual values, whether for enjoyment or for advancement, is valid, always with the exception of England, which generally does not produce intellectual values and with the corruption of whose other 'cultural products' we have already become acquainted.

The talk of the 'connection' of these two 'ethnically related' nations, the English and the Germans, will hopefully finally be silenced. There is nothing more stupid than that. The English are not only fully foreign to our character in the same way that all the other nations are. They can also not complement us in any sense or enrich or please us

---

6   *Maximen und Reflexionen*, Fünfte Abteilung.

with their culture—as the Slavic, Romance, North Germanic, Celtic nations still do.

But now there are people who do not wish to see the relations of the different nations among one another restricted to such sorts of 'stimuli' or 'enrichments' of their own national culture, who rather hope for something like a European or Western European cultural community to which then a new human type, European man, the 'good European', is supposed to correspond. It is not superficial minds that nourish this hope and especially expect from this war that it will bring us one step forward on the way to the European man. Their leader is Nietzsche, who, as we know, coined the catchphrase 'we good Europeans' and whose 'Superman' perhaps points in this direction. This 'good European', whom the individuals restrict territorially in different ways, which, however, is not under consideration here, would therefore, in a strict sense, not be a German, a Frenchman or an Englishman but a German+Frenchman+Englishman divided by three. An inter-, that is, intra-, or, if one prefers, a supra-national man.

I consider this idea of a European man to be basically perverse. The entire idea is, it seems to me, wrongly thought out, as the following considerations make clear.

The construction of a 'European man' as the goal of our development goes back, like all fully or partially 'humanitarian ideals' that inform German souls (insofar as they are not anchored in Christian views), to the ideas of humanity of our 'Weimar thinkers'. Among the latter it was Herder especially who had developed this idea: that it is the highest duty of every man on earth to approximate to his 'idealistic man', that is, to his own God-like idea. That—and not something quite superficial, as was later made of it under the influence of Western Europeans—is the sense of the concept of humanity among those noble minds. 'I wished', says Herder,

> that I could encompass in the word 'humanity' all that I had said up to then about the noble formation of man to reason and freedom, to finer senses and instincts, to the tenderest and strongest health, to the replenishing and

CHAPTER TWELVE. WE AND THE OTHERS

conquest of the earth; for man has no nobler word for his destiny than himself, in whom the image of the creator of our earth lives imprinted to the degree that it can become visible here.[7]

But already the men of those days must have been able to perceive that the membership of man in the different nations produced fully divergent minds and characters. We remember what Schiller, what Wilhelm von Humboldt were already able to declare about the significance of the national in human education. Basically, Herder's *Ideen* itself already went beyond to a discovery of the different national individualities. And his well-known statement: 'Culture moves ahead, but it does not become more perfect for that,'[8] contradicted the common conception of the 'progress of the human race'.

Humboldt maintained already that, through the fine development of language, philosophy and art, the individuality and difference of individual nations would increase, the deeper understanding of different nations would become more difficult. This conviction has since then strengthened itself increasingly among those with deep insight. The members of different nations have, as it were, become special types. And, just as there is no abstract tree elsewhere than in our own imagination, there is also no abstract man as an idea, to approximate to which could be the duty of national men. It would mean destroying all human values if one wished to mix or obliterate the national peculiarities. Every man can perfect himself only within the scope of his national character. The German, the Frenchman, the Englishman can elevate themselves to super-Germans, super-Frenchmen, super-Englishmen, but never to a Superman, and therefore also not to a 'European'. How could that happen? Let us take the contradictions of the English and the German national spirit. The Englishman thinks

---

7 Herder, *Ideen zur Philosophie der Geschichte der Menschheit* (1784–1791), IV. Johann Gottfried Herder (1744–1803) was a major German thinker of the classical period, whose output included works on literature, theology and cultural history.

8 Herder, *Ideen*, XV.

in a trader's way, the German in a heroic: and the third that should arise from the two? He cannot think half in a trader's way and half in a heroic, or if he did that, that would mean an elevation of the English but a lowering of the German. The third man can subscribe to the higher worldview, the heroic, and comprehend the latter increasingly deeply: then he would be indeed not a third man but he would be a man risen beyond the earlier German. Even more unthinkable would a meta-national Superman be as the creator of artistic values. In what language then should the Superman, who is not a German nor an Englishman, compose poetry? Perhaps in Esperanto? I wish him good luck.

Did Nietzsche himself not destroy his ideal image of the meta-national 'good European' with the words of Zarathustra:

> But there were a thousand goals up to now, for there were thousands of nations. Only the fetter around the thousand necks is still missing, there is still lacking the one goal. Mankind still has no goal.
>
> But tell me, my brothers: if mankind still lacks a goal, is it itself not missing also?[9]

No. We must eradicate from our souls also the last remnants of the old ideal of a progressive development of 'mankind'. There is no 'progress' from nation to nation to a higher level; we have not 'progressed' further than the Greeks, if we do not take the concept of progress merely as an engineering concept. Rather, God operates in the different national individualities that 'progress' in themselves, that is, they perfect their own character, approximate more closely to their idea, just as the individual man can progress in his lifetime by being able to bring his natural existence closer to the ideal man within himself. Within every nation there operates a certain vital force that strives for development and realises the character of this nation in its history. The individual nations grow, bloom and wither like flowers in the garden of God:

---

9   *Thus Spake Zarathustra*, I, 'The Thousand and One Goals'.

that alone we can recognise as the meaning of the development of mankind. And the idea of mankind, thus the idea of humanity, cannot be understood differently in its deepest sense than that it reaches its highest and richest outcome in individual noble nations.

These are then the representatives of the idea of God on earth; these are the chosen peoples. That was what the Greeks, the Jews, were. And the chosen people of this century are the Germans.

Why they are that should be proven by this short work; because they believe in a heroic worldview and they alone at this time possess the idea of God on earth.

But we understand also why the other nations persecute us with their hatred; they do not understand us, but they feel our enormous spiritual superiority. In this way were the Jews hated in antiquity because they were the governors of God on earth as long as they alone had adopted in their mind the abstract idea of God. And they went with heads raised high, with a contemptuous smile on their lips, through the swarm of peoples of their age, on whom they looked down with disdain from their proud heights. They closed themselves also off from all foreign character through fear that the sacredness that they bore within themselves might be contaminated through contact with infidels. In this way did the Greeks live among the barbarians in their best days.

So too should the Germans go through the world in our age, proud, with raised heads, in the certain feeling of being God's people. Just as the German bird, the eagle, hovers above all the animals of this earth, so should the German feel himself elevated above all nations that surround him and that he views below him at an infinite depth.

But *noblesse oblige* is valid here too. The idea of being the chosen people burdens us with heavy duties—and only duties. We must, above all, maintain ourselves in the world as a strong nation. We do not set out on the conquest of the world. Have no fear, dear neighbours: we will not swallow you up. What should we do with these indigestible portions in our stomach? And our desire is also not to conquer half-civilised or savage nations to fill them with the German spirit. Such a 'Germanisation' is not possible at all. The Englishman can indeed colonise in this sense and fill foreign peoples with his spirit. He indeed has no spirit. Except the trader's spirit. I can make any man at all a trader and expanding English civilisation is no great wonder. The great 'colonial talent' praised in the English is nothing but an expression of their spiritual poverty. But to implant German culture in other peoples, who would like to undertake that? One cannot install heroism like gaslights in any place you like on earth. We Germans therefore will always remain bad colonisers — and rightly so! And to accumulate foreign countries as England does, that too seems not worth the effort to us. The 'expansionist tendency' therefore does not reside at all in the new Germany. That we leave without envy to England, which has it just as every warehouse does — rightly!

We wish to be and remain a strong German nation and thus a strong state and thus also grow within the limits of the organic. And, if it is necessary that we extend our territorial possession so that the greater national body may obtain space to develop itself, we shall take as much land for ourselves as seems necessary. We shall also set foot where it seems important to us for strategic reasons to maintain our inviolable strength; we shall, therefore, if it benefits our position of power on earth, establish naval bases in Dover, Malta and the Suez. Nothing more. We do not wish to 'expand' at all. For we have more important things to do. We have to develop our own spiritual character, maintain the German soul pure, have to see that the enemy, the trader's mentality, does not penetrate anywhere into our mind, not from outside nor from inside. But this task is an enormous one filled with responsibility. For we know what is at stake: Germany is the last dam against the slime-flood of commercialism that has either already poured over all other countries or is in the process of doing so unstoppably because none of the latter is protected against the advancing danger by the heroic worldview that alone, as we have seen, promises rescue and protection.

May these words enter your hearts, my dear young friends to whom I dedicate these pages and strengthen in you the spirit that will lead us to victory: the German heroic spirit! We, who cannot fight with you in your ranks, look enviously on you who can seal your heroism with your death. We cannot do anything else but forge swords for you with which, on your return to the homeland, you should conduct the great battle against the internal and external enemies of your spiritual heroism.

May this work contribute to convincing you of the mission that you must fulfil and that only you can fulfil!

> The worth of mankind is given into your hand
>
> Preserve it!
>
> It will sink with you, or rise with you ...[10]

---

10 Schiller, 'Die Künstler' (The Artists).

OTHER BOOKS PUBLISHED BY ARKTOS

Sri Dharma Pravartaka Acharya	*The Dharma Manifesto*
Joakim Andersen	*Rising from the Ruins: The Right of the 21st Century*
Winston C. Banks	*Excessive Immigration*
Alain de Benoist	*Beyond Human Rights*
	Carl Schmitt Today
	The Indo-Europeans
	Manifesto for a European Renaissance
	On the Brink of the Abyss
	The Problem of Democracy
	Runes and the Origins of Writing
	View from the Right (vol. 1–3)
Arthur Moeller van den Bruck	*Germany's Third Empire*
Matt Battaglioli	*The Consequences of Equality*
Kerry Bolton	*Revolution from Above*
	Yockey: A Fascist Odyssey
Isac Boman	*Money Power*
Ricardo Duchesne	*Faustian Man in a Multicultural Age*
Alexander Dugin	*Ethnos and Society*
	Ethnosociology
	Eurasian Mission
	The Fourth Political Theory
	Last War of the World-Island
	Political Platonism
	Putin vs Putin
	The Rise of the Fourth Political Theory
Edward Dutton	*Race Differences in Ethnocentrism*
Mark Dyal	*Hated and Proud*
Clare Ellis	*The Blackening of Europe*
Koenraad Elst	*Return of the Swastika*
Julius Evola	*The Bow and the Club*
	Fascism Viewed from the Right
	A Handbook for Right-Wing Youth
	Metaphysics of Power
	Metaphysics of War
	The Myth of the Blood
	Notes on the Third Reich
	The Path of Cinnabar
	Recognitions

OTHER BOOKS PUBLISHED BY ARKTOS

	A Traditionalist Confronts Fascism
Guillaume Faye	*Archeofuturism*
	Archeofuturism 2.0
	The Colonisation of Europe
	Convergence of Catastrophes
	Ethnic Apocalypse
	A Global Coup
	Prelude to War
	Sex and Deviance
	Understanding Islam
	Why We Fight
Daniel S. Forrest	*Suprahumanism*
Andrew Fraser	*Dissident Dispatches*
	The WASP Question
Génération Identitaire	*We are Generation Identity*
Peter Goodchild	*The Taxi Driver from Baghdad*
Paul Gottfried	*War and Democracy*
Petr Hampl	*Breached Enclosure*
Porus Homi Havewala	*The Saga of the Aryan Race*
Lars Holger Holm	*Hiding in Broad Daylight*
	Homo Maximus
	Incidents of Travel in Latin America
	The Owls of Afrasiab
Richard Houck	*Liberalism Unmasked*
A. J. Illingworth	*Political Justice*
Alexander Jacob	*De Naturae Natura*
Jason Reza Jorjani	*Faustian Futurist*
	Iranian Leviathan
	Lovers of Sophia
	Novel Folklore
	Prometheism
	Prometheus and Atlas
	World State of Emergency
Henrik Jonasson	*Sigmund*
Vincent Joyce	*The Long Goodbye*
Ruuben Kaalep & August Meister	*Rebirth of Europe*
Roderick Kaine	*Smart and SeXy*
Peter King	*Here and Now*

OTHER BOOKS PUBLISHED BY ARKTOS

	Keeping Things Close
	On Modern Manners
JAMES KIRKPATRICK	*Conservatism Inc.*
LUDWIG KLAGES	*The Biocentric Worldview*
	Cosmogonic Reflections
PIERRE KREBS	*Guillaume Faye: Truths & Tributes*
	Fighting for the Essence
JULIEN LANGELLA	*Catholic and Identitarian*
JOHN BRUCE LEONARD	*The New Prometheans*
STEPHEN PAX LEONARD	*The Ideology of Failure*
	Travels in Cultural Nihilism
WILLIAM S. LIND	*Retroculture*
PENTTI LINKOLA	*Can Life Prevail?*
H. P. LOVECRAFT	*The Conservative*
NORMAN LOWELL	*Imperium Europa*
CHARLES MAURRAS	*The Future of the Intelligentsia*
	& For a French Awakening
JOHN HARMON MCELROY	*Agitprop in America*
MICHAEL O'MEARA	*Guillaume Faye and the Battle of Europe*
	New Culture, New Right
MICHAEL MILLERMAN	*Beginning with Heidegger*
BRIAN ANSE PATRICK	*The NRA and the Media*
	Rise of the Anti-Media
	The Ten Commandments of Propaganda
	Zombology
TITO PERDUE	*The Bent Pyramid*
	Journey to a Location
	Lee
	Morning Crafts
	Philip
	The Sweet-Scented Manuscript
	William's House (vol. 1–4)
RAIDO	*A Handbook of Traditional Living* (vol. 1–2)
STEVEN J. ROSEN	*The Agni and the Ecstasy*
	The Jedi in the Lotus
RICHARD RUDGLEY	*Barbarians*
	Essential Substances
	Wildest Dreams

OTHER BOOKS PUBLISHED BY ARKTOS

ERNST VON SALOMON	*It Cannot Be Stormed*
	The Outlaws
PIERO SAN GIORGIO	*CBRN: Surviving Chemical, Biological, Radiological & Nuclear Events*
	Giuseppe
SRI SRI RAVI SHANKAR	*Celebrating Silence*
	Know Your Child
	Management Mantras
	Patanjali Yoga Sutras
	Secrets of Relationships
GEORGE T. SHAW (ED.)	*A Fair Hearing*
FENEK SOLÈRE	*Kraal*
OSWALD SPENGLER	*Man and Technics*
RICHARD STOREY	*The Uniqueness of Western Law*
TOMISLAV SUNIC	*Against Democracy and Equality*
	Homo Americanus
	Postmortem Report
	Titans are in Town
ASKR SVARTE	*Gods in the Abyss*
HANS-JÜRGEN SYBERBERG	*On the Fortunes and Misfortunes of Art in Post-War Germany*
ABIR TAHA	*Defining Terrorism*
	The Epic of Arya (2nd ed.)
	Nietzsche's Coming God, or the Redemption of the Divine
	Verses of Light
JEAN THIRIART	*Europe: An Empire of 400 Million*
BAL GANGADHAR TILAK	*The Arctic Home in the Vedas*
DOMINIQUE VENNER	*For a Positive Critique*
	The Shock of History
HANS VOGEL	*How Europe Became American*
MARKUS WILLINGER	*A Europe of Nations*
	Generation Identity
ALEXANDER WOLFHEZE	*Alba Rosa*
	Rupes Nigra

Made in the USA
Monee, IL
08 April 2025